C000278326

Marjorie R. Gatland

ONE AND ALL

Two Years
in the Chilterns

ONE AND ALL

Two Years
in the Chilterns

Kenneth Allsop

Foreword by
Richard Mabey

Illustrated by
Gordon Beningfield

ALAN SUTTON

First published in the United Kingdom in 1991 by
Alan Sutton Publishing · Phoenix Mill · Far Thrupp · Stroud · Gloucestershire

First published in the United States of America in 1992 by
Alan Sutton Publishing Inc. · Wolfeboro Falls · NH 03896–0848

British Library Cataloguing in Publication Data
Allsop, Kenneth
One and all.
I. Title
335.941

ISBN 0–86299–966–9

Library of Congress Cataloging in Publication Data
Allsop, Kenneth, 1920–1973.
One and all: a personal chronicle of two years in a community/Kenneth Allsop;
foreword by Richard Mabey.
ISBN 0–86299–966–9
1. Allsop, Kenneth, 1920–1973 — Homes and haunts — Englands — Chiltern
Hills. 2. Chiltern Hills (England) — Description and travel. 3 Country life —
England — Chiltern Hills. 4. Communal living — England — Chiltern Hills.
5. Authors, English — 20th century — Homes and haunts — England —
Chiltern Hills. I. Title.
'R6051.L55054 1992
:28'.91403 — dc20
B}

91–20734
CIP

Typeset in Garamond 12/13.
Typesetting and origination by
Alan Sutton Publishing Limited.
Printed in Great Britain by
WBC Print Limited,
Bridgend, Wales.

Introduction
by Richard Mabey

At the time of his death in 1973, Kenneth Allsop was a household name, a distinguished journalist both in the press and on television. Most evenings he could be seen presenting the current affairs programme *Twenty Four Hours*, an urbane, grey-templed figure touched with just a hint of world-weariness. He had written books on American migrant workers and English Angry Young Men, was a regular reviewer of books and films in the quality newspapers, and had an unashamed fondness for fast cars and jazz. In every way he seemed the epitome of the cultured, metropolitan man.

Yet he is remembered today for another, less public face. Kenneth was also a passionate conservationist, a romantic who revered Richard Jefferies' transcendental writings on nature (and shared some of his melancholy and physical pain), and who half-yearned to be a deep-rooted countryman himself. A few days before his death he had been watching buzzards and red kites in west Wales, and had confided to his wife Betty that he wished he could have his remains left on a hilltop for the birds of prey to dispose of.

Throughout Kenneth's adult life there was a underlying tension between the gregarious urban intellectual and the solitary rural dreamer. Neither role seemed sufficient by itself, nor wholly complementary to the other. Kenneth did not seek escape in nature, so much as a heightened perception, a resolution of paradoxes, a kind of grace. Yet like Richard Jefferies, he simply uncovered more layers of

Kenneth Allsop

contradiction, and found himself guilty of what Jefferies called 'the old, old error: I love the earth and therefore the earth loves me'.

But towards the end of his life he did come close, in many senses, to finding his place. In the late sixties he moved with his family to an ancient mill-house in West Dorset – 'beyond contestation the loveliest part of the United Kingdom . . . the last place left, I think, and the one I love most' – and not long afterwards began a weekly column about life there in the *Daily Mail*. His notes on birds, badgers, Agas, errant pets and Dorset Christmases – all seen through the sympathetic eyes of a literate newcomer – were hugely popular, and the pieces were published in book form in 1972. Twenty years on, *In the Country* remains one of the very few 'country' books to have an authentic late twentieth-century voice, to speak for the growing army of outsiders – the commuters and townee weekenders and avid rural-book readers, all those exiled from the countryside in their lives but not in their hearts.

The road to that spell of near-contentment had been a protracted and at times frustrating one. Twenty years previously, the Allsops had lived for two years in a communal house in the Bedfordshire countryside, and Kenneth had begun his long tussle with the contrary pulls in his life. It was his first sustained spell as a freelance writer as well as a rural communard, and it was a smarting, disappointing experience as much as a fulfillment. *One and All* is his account of those two years. It is a curious book, diffident, contrived in places, evasive about personal relations inside the community and naive when it does confront them. Yet it contains passages of powerful descriptive writing, and revealing insights into Kenneth's developing attitudes towards nature. He had glimpsed its vitality as well as its essential otherness, and his attempts to embrace it as a healing force in his own life are as relevant now as they were then.

Kenneth was born in Yorkshire in 1920 and brought up as an only child by a mother who despised any displays of affection. He became an introspective young man, a devotee of Jefferies' and Henry Williamson's nature writings, and when he left school at seventeen went directly into a job on a local newspaper. He never went to university, and was called up to the RAF in 1940. During the war he had a leg amputated because of surgical TB, and spent two years in hospital. These losses – of a limb, a higher education and perhaps what he saw as his youth — fused into a sense of pain and resentment that never entirely left him, and drove him to work and play with furious intensity. To walk with him over his beloved Dorset hills, and see his face grey with pain at the effort, was an awesome lesson in both courage and obstinacy.

He was demobbed in 1946, and exhausted by years of ill health, went to ground with Betty in a bed-sit in north London, and took a succession of hack journalistic jobs. The atmosphere of those post-war years is caught with a bleak accuracy in the opening pages, and the counter-attractions of the commune founded by two friends from the short-lived Common Wealth party are obvious. At first the Allsops felt too poor and insecure to join, but in 1948 Kenneth's first book was accepted for publication. *Adventure Lit Their Star* is a novel about the struggles of a rare wading bird, the little ringed plover, to establish itself as a breeding species in Outer London. It remains one of Kenneth's most powerful and heartfelt works (it received the 1949 John Llewelyn Rhys Memorial Prize), and it is hard to say whether he identified more with these indomitable birds which were scraping a living in the scruffy landscape of gravel pits and wasteland west of Heathrow Airport, or with the invalided RAF man who watched them. But the success of the book gave him and Betty the confidence (and finances) to join the community in 1948.

Barwythe (called Bereworde here) was a Queen Anne manor house in the northern reaches of the Chilterns, a landscape that was, rather aptly, like a gentle foretaste of the Dorset hill-country in which he was eventually to find a haven. The community consisted of a shifting pattern of some eight families, mostly from professional, middle-class backgrounds, and committed to socialism in a rather abstract way. They had a progressive, Reichian approach towards child-rearing but not much else in the way of a philosophy, and by modern standards it was a quaintly old-fashioned and illiberal community. The women did the housework and the children ate separately from their parents. It was not so much a commune as a group of like-minded families living under the same roof for convenience.

One and All documents their daily round, and tells us something of the forces that eventually led to the break-up of the group. It was a predictable mixture: trouble with the locals, who were suspicious of Barwythians' politics and attitudes towards children; problems over money; disagreements about policy, decision-making and discipline. But Kenneth was never very good at handling or portraying personal relationships, and these passages – especially those on child upbringing – are awkward and naive. His daughter Amanda (born just before the move to Barwythe) comments on this in her fine introduction to a collection of their correspondence:

> [his mother] would certainly have insisted upon a similar restraint of feeling from him. Added to that was his inwardly directed – perhaps self-absorbed – mind, and the two working together caused his basic difficulties in communicating, especially with small children, who obviously hadn't learned to converse intellectually, nor to follow accepted codes and rules of superficial social conversation. He couldn't relate to the irrational mechanic of children's minds, and was always scared of them and uncomfortable with them. (*Letters to his Daughter*, ed. Amanda Allsop, 1974)

Kenneth's ambivalent attitudes towards authority and freedom percolate even the descriptive nature writing in *One and All*. He admires both wild countryside and countryside which bears the intricate marks of human occupation. He rails against the casual clear-felling of a beechwood, yet composes a long, almost Whitmanesque celebration of the felling of an ancient cherry for firewood. He writes poignantly of the landscape round Barwythe, 'a country of ancient pattern, a pattern that had been evolved by tyranny, infliction, often ruthless cruelty'. Yet he admits he loves the intricate mosaic that resulted, and frequently uses squirearchical jargon in his writing.

This fascination with specialized languages, like his habit of slightly disguising place names (rather weakly excused as preserving 'a modicum of secrecy' in *In the Country*) was part of the emotional detachment described by his daughter. His writing often seems distant, tightly reined, an obsessional chore more than a spontaneous pleasure. Yet in *One and All* it is already starting to show an eclectic mixing of styles, that unique brew of Romanticism, condensed journalese, scientific argot and Raymond Chandler that was to become his trademark.

The urban rhythms in his prose were also a deliberate device. Just as he rejoiced when the natural world penetrated human redoubts (there are marvellous cameos of badgers triumphing over bulldozers, and a tree-creeper burrowing out a roost in a giant American redwood), so he thought that nature could be seen all the more richly through sophisticated eyes. But he saw this blurring of barriers as a risky, double-edged business. Belief in nature's resilience could lead to a kind of complacency. And an over-intellectualised view of the natural world could rob it, precisely, of its restorative 'naturalness'.

One spring-like January day, he escapes from the community chores that had become increasingly irksome to him, and finds himself watching duck at the nearby Tring Reservoirs. He gives rapturous descriptions of the ducks' evening flight and tries to reach a child-like 'immersion in the day and the hour'. But like many writers before him he realizes it is an impossible dream, and that the self-awareness that made such a hope possible would prevent it ever being fulfilled. At the end of the book, walking round an empty Barwythe, he rejoices to see the spotted flycatchers, his favourite summer birds, back in occupation, symoblizing the continuity of history and nature, 'the enduring values'.

Later in 1950 Kenneth took a job on *Picture Post*; followed by a succession of increasingly responsible positions on national newspapers, and finally on television. But unqualified happiness eluded him. The pain in his stump gnawed; the world got filthier; his missed university years still rankled, though the short-term Fellowship he was awarded at Merton College, Oxford (he was studying the relations between the pre-war 'Open Air' cults and the rise of Fascism) did much to soften his bitterness. But he still felt excluded from the official networks of power and knowledge, and was deeply hurt (though not surprised) when his pioneering and hard-hitting environmental TV series *Down to Earth* trod on too many important toes and was exiled for a second series to a poorly-equipped studio in the provinces.

He did a good deal of writing and broadcasting on environmental issues in the early seventies, much of it celebrating the dogged, inventive and inspiring survival of nature in hostile surroundings (his film about the wildlife of New York city remains a classic). Yet this hid a deep pessimism about the future of the planet, and a growing fear that there was an even bleaker prospect than ecological catastrophe: that humanity might come to adapt, even enjoy, a 'treeless, neon-lit, profit-geared environment'.

But there was solace in Dorset, and many of the themes and images that first saw the light at Barwythe reached a marvellous fruition in his weekly celebrations of Wessex life: the reassurance of summer flycatchers, the ancient continuities and conviviality of Christmas, the excitement of walking out and just letting things happen. There was even philosophical comfort of a kind, in settling for a modest niche like the rest of creation. Writing of the mill's history he reflected that 'to be included in the long, uncalled roll is a privilege which is both enhancing and humbling: you are merely another entry on that densely-layered palimpsest, and that is sufficient.'

But it was not sufficient for long. The accumulated pains eventually proved too much, and on 23 May 1973 he took his own life. It was entirely typical of him that the brave, level-headed and almost maddeningly matter-of-fact letter he left for Betty included a fond reference to the peregrine falcons they had just watched, and a very black joke about his missed TV deadline being less important than the one he had just kept.

Selected Bibliography

1949, *Adventure Lit Their Star*; new edition, 1962; paperback edition 1972.

1958, *The Angry Decade* ('a study of the cultural revolt of the nineteen fifties').

1959, *Rare Bird* (a novel).

1965, *Scan* (selected criticism).

1967, *Hard Travellin'* ('the hobo and his history').

1970, *Fit To Live In?* (educational textbook on 'the future of Britain's countryside').

1972, *In the Country*; paperback edition, 1974.

1974, *Letters To His Daughter*, ed. Amanda Allsop.

Names and Places

═══

Family Names

Bee   Betty Allsop, Kenneth's wife
Andrew, Roo   Tristan Allsop, their elder son
Amanda, Mandy   Amanda Allsop, their daughter

Place Names

Ashcroft Park   Ashridge Park
Bereworde   Barwythe Hall
Boxwood   Boxmoor, near Hemel Hempstead
Buckwood Estate   Beechwood Estate
Burkstead   Berkhamstead, Hertfordshire
Downsteeple   Dunstable, Bedfordshire
Estodham   Studham, Bedfordshire
Gedd (Valley and River)   Gade
Horsemoor Green   Langley, near Slough
Little Gadeley   Little Gaddesden, Hertfordshire

Chapter One

Two letters came that day in the middle of February 1946, delivered to that melancholy villa in Highgate – not Highgate of the hill but the dismal valley north of the Archway Road, a plexus of *Spion Kops*, *The Laurelses*, besooted privets and windows darkly secretive with cream net.

One said that the features job was mine; the other said did we want to join the community? There they were, the lusted-after irreconcilables, clashing so neatly on the same morning, leaving it to us to sort out the tantalizing intertwistings of coincidence.

The origins were wide apart. The first sequence began on the day that I swung out of hospital on crutches, leaving my right leg a faint scattering of ashes in the internal crevices of the furnace. That was a fluid, bitter period. Behind were the barren, unhappy years of the RAF, and all that had forced up out of that stony soil and withered: the two novels written in barracks rooms and wireless cabins, and hawked around publishers' offices in Bloomsbury during leaves, and, quite justly, rejected; the determination not to return to the journalism of 1937–40; the resolve, while sitting in a NAAFI and reading a pamphlet about the Government course in forestry for ex-servicemen, to cut a new path in the post-war world. Legless, I sat in the upper-floor flat of the Highgate villa, looking out on to the scabrous lawn and prowling in my thoughts, like the churchyard haunter whom guidebooks cater for, among the graves of those pathetic juvenile aspirations. It was a situation that had to be faced. I faced it, first by smoking over my typewriter all day during the hours Bee was at the bookshop, torturing words out of myself to form dead, artificial articles and stories — that always came back. That lasted less than a month. I came to a decision in an explosion of desperation. If I was now physically incapable of doing anything on farm or in forest, if it meant journalism again, then the start had to be made immediately. I could not go on mouldering month after month, waiting for my name to jerk slowly to the top of the limitless list of candidates for Roehampton tin legs. In a suitcase full of papers I found my old National Union of Journalists card, with its embarrassing photograph of my 18-year-old self trying to look like a reporter. I stumped down the stairs into the hall, and there, with an aspidistra licking my neck with its linoleum tongue, I telephoned the Union office.

They were understanding and helpful. Later that day they rang back with the suggestion of an immobile job, which I got, sub-editing for one of the magazines of a gargantuan London publishing house. At first I had been exalted. Just to set out each morning at a regular time to catch the bus was a mystical experience, like having a guide-line slipped out of the darkness into your groping hand. Yet that happiness did not last long. Before a few weeks had passed I knew that basically the situation had not changed. I felt trapped, back in the same little pen only now with my crutches as an additional fence. The job in itself had no attraction for me; I hated the way we lived in the squalid dark rooms; I wanted to escape from London, to get into the country and stay there; and Bee was pregnant. My discontent and the stewed down-at-heel respectability of Clarendon Road did not seem to me to be a good atmosphere for the child to come into.

But, until the winter of 1945, it looked as if life was going to stay as it had crystallized, hard and dull. Then there developed something that, although outside the periphery of my uncertain ideals, suggested a partial solution. A newspaper friend whom I had worked with before the war had gone, after demobilization, to a weekly paper twenty miles out of London as news editor. He mentioned during a meeting that when newsprint supplies increased the paper would expand its features side: did that arouse my interest? There opened the prospect of leaving London, of living at least within walking distance of fields and trees, and of work of greater variety than being hunched all day over a desk passing an endless belt of copy through my hands. I had by now been equipped with my leg. Clankingly awkward and sore in the groin though I was, I felt capable of a more energetic life, and I told him, gratefully, that I was interested, very. I had an interview with the editor, then six months passed until, abruptly, the letter of confirmation came.

The sequence that led up to the other letter had been vaguer and had had an earlier beginning. It was when Bee, during my two years in hospital, had canalized everything of herself into the whirlpool of politics. She had joined the Common Wealth election 'circus', the name given by the *Daily Express* to Sir Richard Acland's shock troops. It was during the 1945 General Election campaign that the community idea was first put to her. Her candidate was Ian Parfitt, a solicitor, then a flight-lieutenant in the RAF. On a squally night as they plodded across moorland from one village to another in 'Policy', the Election Austin Seven – so named because it was apt to swerve from left to right – he told her that after his discharge he and his wife Anna hoped to found a community where a number of like-minded families could live together co-operatively, and, by means of pooled efforts domestically, obtain the time and opportunity for experimenting with a more sensible way of living. It sounded, in general terms, attractive to Bee and she told Ian that if ever it developed we would like to hear about it.

Ian did not get in then and it had not been until late in the autumn of 1945 that we heard from Anna asking if we would like to spend a Sunday at their Stanmore flat to talk over the community idea with them and some friends. We went along, taking sandwiches for an indoor picnic lunch. There were about a dozen people there. We knew three: Martin Larkin, a delicate, slight man with wispy fair hair who had just returned to publishing after five years as a stoker in the Navy, his wife Elaine, who had been an active Common Wealther, and Julian, Anna's brother, who after leaving the RAF had also been a Common Wealth agent, but the others, apart from Anna and Ian, were strangers. There was a lot of talking, and many theories and arguments, some of them pronouncedly outlandish, were advanced; yet, broadly, Bee and I found ourselves entering enthusiastically into the scheme. Particularly I liked the setting that was proposed, a manor house or an old rectory on the fringe of a village, and the new freedom that the scheme seemed to promise.

Then, it was still at the germinating stage. Ian and Anna were feeling their way, assessing how many and what sort of families might be prepared to join in. Finally it was decided that Anna and Elaine should canvass estate agents to see what properties were available.

During the next few months there were spasmodic telephone contacts. We heard that a house here, a house there, had been visited: that it was too dear, too inaccessible, too big, too something. Gradually what had been an expectation faded into a pale possibility, and eventually was almost forgotten.

Then the letter came. Or rather it was a note, from Anna, saying that they had found what they were sure was the very place, that it was a good-looking Queen Anne manor standing in thirty acres of ground in the Eastern Chilterns, and that, the next Sunday, prospective candidates were meeting at Boxwood station for a day's on-the-spot conference. Did we still want to join the community, and if so would we turn up on Sunday?

Our reaction was one of controlled consternation. Our waned enthusiasm waxed full and bright – but it was instantly obvious that this could not dovetail with the course of action that the other letter of that morning opened. One could not work on a local paper and live thirty miles away. In any case my wage would not be big enough. Over breakfast I read the duplicated statement, prepared for the scores of people who had answered the advertisement in the *New Statesman*, *Tribune* and *Common Wealth Review*, that Anna had enclosed.

We aim to live in real country, but near enough to 'belong' to a village. About an hour from a London terminus, preferably on the north or west side of Town. The type of house we think will prove most suitable is a long, low Georgian one (enough ground floor living-rooms with garden access for children); 10 acres upwards; about 20 bedrooms; orchard; company's water and electricity; several cottages; many bathrooms; and Aga or Esse cooker. The price freehold (judging from the houses we have seen, and approximate incomes and running costs) should be between £8,000 and £10,000. If a few of us raise enough capital it is hoped to include others paying their share in the form of rent. We estimate that the maximum of from £150 to £200 per family per annum will cover mortgage repayments (rent), rates, water, light, heat, central heating and a contribution to one full-time gardener. The expenses of a Montessori teacher, cook and other help in house and garden will depend upon the possibility of their being part of the community, but obviously, shared, would not be high.

Communal meals will, we believe, be preferred, but for any one who wants to, there are always housemaids' pantries easily convertible into kitchenettes. A common-room will, we feel, be much used by us all, and gramophone recitals, discussions, and such communal activities be frequent. Each family will have its bathroom. Other details depend largely on the house and on ourselves as it is impossible to be more explicit as yet.

At the moment we have five families, ages range from 25 to 40, nine children (between us all I hasten to add), aged from three weeks to six years. Most of us hope to have more. Several other people may want to join in, but have no capital and for other reasons can't decide now. There will be no shortage of tenants, even congenial ones, as we have received over 40 letters this week – of which yours is one.

This is to be an attempt at new ways of living together, a community to which each shall make his contribution, and which will provide a far richer background, for children and for adults alike, than any one family alone can give.

About ourselves. Briefly, jobs include book publishers, solicitor, election agent, documentary film-maker. Interests and hobbies range through European literature, classical music, swing, ballet, education, psychology, nature cure, natural child birth, gardening, ducks and poultry keeping, and so on. Most of us are socialists, and our sense of humour level is, I think, high. Now if you are still interested, let us meet at once and see if we find each other bearable.

There was a certain mistiness about it that left me unsatisfied. It was a concept that attracted and stimulated me but part of me was held back by a suspicion that it might be just a little too pottery-weavery in a William Morris way. Yet it shone with a faith in people, for was not that the base on which the structure was to be built? I was twenty-six and one month, and I was idealistic. Strangely enough the war had increased my idealism after a period following Dunkirk when everything seemed to be a gigantic confidence trick. The germination of those ideals had occurred just before the war, when I was a 17-year-old cub reporter on a weekly paper. Two things propagated their growth. One day I stood on the pavement in the London suburban town where I was working and for half an hour watched an army pass. It was an army of men in worn-out shoes and caps and grimy cheap suits, whose faces were grey with lack of food and sunlight, set with exhaustion. They were Welsh hunger-marchers, men compressed to such depths of desperation that they put their degradation on display in an attempt to shame the smug and the privileged into humanity. The sight of the marchers had a profound effect upon me. Unemployment until then had been something that existed, a natural part of England of the '30s, something that *was*, like oxygen or electricity or Australia. I accepted the statement of the authorities that it did exist, but it was invisible, without any personal meaning. Now, suddenly, a personal responsibility had been thrust upon me and it was a painful, bewildering awareness that flooded into the emptiness. It was only a day or two later that I was sent to report a concert at the Public Hall. A troupe of Basque children were giving a programme of traditional songs and dances. On its merits as entertainment it was spectacular. After the drear misery of so many amateur shows, precocious bubble-curled little girls tap-dancing and singing in arch tinny voices, and self-conscious societies struggling vainly with *The Barretts of Wimpole Street*, here was colour, reality, vitality. For two hours I sat entranced watching those dark-skinned children with their blue-black eyes and sparkling teeth, singing their vehement Spanish songs and dancing with a fury of gaiety which was untinged by the bitterness of each one's personal tragedy. Afterwards I talked to them with the help of the men and women who were sponsoring the show, which was to raise funds for a refugee committee. All were orphans. Their parents, their homes, their hometown lives had been extinguished in the Civil War. Until that moment the Spanish War had, like unemployment, been a vague and meaningless thing. My eyes had glided over the headlines without absorbing an impression of any kind. Why the war was being fought, who was fighting it, I had only the slenderest notion.

The combination of those two events was revelationary. Suddenly I became alive to the realities of the times I was living in. My mind had been obedient to its conditioning at school, where we were taught not to mix with the grammar school boys down the road. Somewhere George Orwell pointed out that the average Conservative is Conservative less for argued-out economic reasons than for the indisputable fact that poor people smell. That had roughly been my outlook. Now I could not quickly enough throw out the prejudices and superstitions that had been stuffed into my brain since childhood until the desirable state of intellectual suffocation had been achieved. I wanted to flush away the stale atmosphere of bourgeois lassitude in which I had lived with the harsh, cold air of actuality. In a way, perhaps I had been temperamentally oriented towards this happening, for as a child I had always fiercely sided with the Redskins of film and story. The strenuous propaganda which thickly daubed the settlers and cowboys holy, and the Redskin satanic, did not bluff me. It was the Redskins' country. Why should they allow themselves to be ousted without shooting off a few flaming arrows and capturing scalps in consolation? Or perhaps it was merely the fact that the Sioux and Blackfeet invariably suffered defeat that called up my sympathetic support for them.

However, at the age of seventeen I began to call myself a socialist. I read avidly of Blatchford and *Tribune* and Left Book Club editions, and I became a throaty champion of the International Brigade and the Republican cause. I even contemplated enlisting, but at that time I had not sufficiently uncoiled myself from the tentacles of the past; I could not make the decision. My attitude was essentially an emotional one, and I still think that is a better reason for being a socialist than one of detached, clinical, Fabianesque rationalization. To read of the Tolpuddle Martyrs or the Jarrow destitute or the Scottsboro Boys moved me to tears. Behind those tears was a passionate desire to suffer, to experience and to act.

The war was a sledgehammer blow. It was too complex a problem to be understood. 'We are fighting fascism' was a slogan soon jettisoned – it was too much of an abstraction. 'We are fighting a war' became the theme. We were at war; we had to win. We had to save our skins. It was magnificently simple if one could be matter-of-fact and content with a short-term view, or better still, with no view at all. I could not be content with that. I wanted to believe it was a just war, and all the day-to-day convolutions of politics and policy seemed to disprize that principle. There were the superficial, customary 'good times', but I was miserable and frustrated underneath. During training periods at a station near High Wycombe I wrote a novel, sitting on a palliasse in my corner of the hut, scribbling in Signal Office Diaries. In it I tried to regain belief in a purity of ideals. It was the story of three men, a farm labourer, an industrial worker, a journalist, who entered the war from the hollow, purposeless cynicism of the thirties and found fulfilment and dedication in the war. They died together in the desert, with the knowledge of having found their star. It was a bad novel, bad because really I had not believed what I was writing, and I knew I did not believe it as I wrote. It was an attempt to convince myself, and the argument succeeded no better because I put it into the mouths of imagined characters. After that there was blankness, a deliberate deadening of the frustration that blighted everything I had had faith in. Often I climbed the fence at the rear of the camp and walked for miles over the Chiltern hills, wrapping myself round like a cocoon with the skin of those windy April days. Finding a long-tailed tit's nest in a bramble hung like a fishing net down a worked-out overgrown stone quarry, exploring the great hangars of beech, watching a kestrel steering its shadow across the pliant turf of a naked drum of land, stepping between clumps of primroses, enormous as bowls of fruit, in the splintered sunshine of a hazel wood – these were the things that I wound around me in sensitized layers.

A year or so passed and the mood lengthened into an established cynical state of mind. Then I heard of Acland. I read his yellow-jacketed book *What It Will Be Like* and the lock gates were swung open. All the confined weight of disillusionment flooded out. I read, stumbling with haste, 'We must create a new social atmosphere, we must think ourselves in a new way, we must live for new motives. We must become new people.' It seemed to me to be salvation. Here was a man who believed in the phoenix. He was sitting in the ruins drawing plans, and when I read his plan my old passions and yearnings returned and instantly formed a pattern and I saw that, after all, they could be possible. In my myopia I had thought that the war was the end – 'the whimper' *and* 'the bang'. Acland was a visionary and he had seen that it could be exploited for good, that, in fact, its revolutionary ruthlessness had in a few years bulldozed out thickets of reaction and opposition that would have taken decades of gradual reform. With Bee – we had recently been married – I spent an evening of leave listening to Acland speak at a meeting, and his sparrowhawk quickness, his fervency and his clarity were for me confirmation.

Eight years later when I met Acland again he seemed to have lost his inner combustion and compulsion. The same personality, the same manner, actions, words, yet they seemed to have changed, to have become automatic reactions to a set formula. But I could not be sure that it was not I who had changed. Common Wealth had dropped like a shooting star into darkness. With the Labour Party in power, the theory went, an independent, and in effect opposition socialist force was superfluous. All energy must be deflected to the main stream. Crusading now had become a practical job of work, and the place for the conscientious socialist was within the Labour Party, strengthening and enriching it. I was not sure about that. With the dissolution of Common Wealth and the return to old balances, a despair-tinged uncertainty had revived. I was beginning to tire of politics, of the laboured, niggling, nose-to-paper work that it meant on an every-day level. I wanted Jerusalem on Blake's terms, not on the terms of envelope-addressing, canvassing, interminable committee wrangling and winter-night meetings in dim three-quarter-empty back-street halls. They were debasements, cinders on a fire, they dulled the flame and distorted the vision. And, of course, they were necessary.

Perhaps this was partly the reason why I wanted to be part of the community. That would be a microcosm, one would be bringing the pamphlets and the orators' words to life. It was a short cut. But that was only a factor. My political enthusiasm ebbed and flowed, and was more often at ebb-tide now. It was writing that obsessed me. There was never a day that I did not experience that sick feeling in my stomach, as if my intestines were being tightly rolled like a ball of knitting wool. It was a feeling that drove me to my desk to release words on to paper. At that time I was always beginning, rarely finishing, but it was essential to write, and to go a few days without writing produced a harrowing, relentless guilt.

As I read through Anna's outline my mind excitedly created a picture, a composite of desirable things: taking part in a fascinating experiment, living in the country, and writing against a background of comradeship and the truthfulness of the natural world. I knew little about communities. D.H. Lawrence had longed to start one, I remembered, an island of indifference to the material world, which was to have been in Sicily, Florida, Mexico, Cornwall, but his dream had to the end remained a dream. There was an old-established colony of 'simple-lifers' at Whiteway, in the Gloucestershire Cotswolds, I had heard. And there were, of course, the *Bruderhof* communities. But the fine details of the life lived in such places could be supplied only by my imagination. Every community would organically develop its own character, I assumed. Who could say what ours would be like?

'But is it worth going down to this place on Sunday?' I said disconsolately to Bee while I chewed toast and marmalade. 'I can't see how we could join in. Oh, why do things always have to happen in the most complicated way?'

'Never mind. We'll go and think about that afterwards,' Bee said calmly. 'We might be able to work something out.'

That was Bee's normal outlook. She had a summer-day serenity that remained, outwardly at least, undisturbed at times of trouble and crisis, and a sense of immediacy which prevented her efforts being negated by apprehension and a feeling of futility. Whereas I fought out my battles in anguished detail before they began. Having decided that defeat was inevitable, I was drop-jawed with surprised pleasure if I succeeded. It was a frame of mind that had been transformed from a tendency into a trait by my two years in hospital. Hopes had been kicked down so often, disaster had followed disaster so unrelievedly, that optimism and faith had become in my eyes the stupid innocence of a fool. Since then a bleakness of outlook had become a characteristic and the seeds of doom were apparent to me in most things. I drew on her for confidence like a tap.

We went on the Sunday. The train from Euston thrust northwards through the embroiled squalor of Outer London. It was not easy to be sure where a bomb had dropped. The rubbly gaps harmonized so well with the universality of desolation. The brief interruption of the Green Belt and then the semi-detached eczema of Watford and Abbots Langley. Boxwood, and we were walking down the platform glancing furtively at people who carried rucksacks and looked interesting enough to be community candidates. I went down the steps in cautious stiff-legged lunges. I was not yet fully in control of the monstrous hinged metal apparatus that was strapped around me. At the bottom a clot of uncomfortable looking people were being herded together by Ian and Anna. Two big square hire cars were drawn up. Bee and I were packed into one with a group we had never before seen. None of them, as it happened, did ultimately join the community.

My sight was restricted to a narrow angled view between someone's back and someone else's head. All I saw of Boxwood was a jerky succession of buildings and then there was the moist looking green of open February country streaming by. After about twenty minutes the car turned sharply and we began climbing, up and up a narrow crooked lane, and through the funnel I could see exhilarating limbs of hill-land striding up to a sun-patched sky. I saw a magpie rippling across the lane and a flock of greenfinches flurried up from the low thorn hedge like a burst pillow, with bright flashes of yellow from the cocks. Then the car was slowing, turning through tall wrought-iron gates, clumsily crunching up a curling gravel drive to the edge of which beeches grew. And there were rooks nests in the beeches. We followed the drive's curve and the house came into view.

It was very long, with a deep roof of wine tiles. A golden weathercock twirled flirtatiously upon a mast. There was a door, double doors, of oak set within a wide stone arch. Jackdaws flew yelping from the tall stacks, and as we got out of the cars the rooks rose from their colony nests in a swirling, roaring cloud.

Martin's dachshund spurted about the oval gravel turning circle, his nose first scooping along like a snow-plough, then weaving about in the air gathering up the strange, exciting, rich new scents. In a more restrained manner we were all doing that. With Martin I walked across to the expanse of grass where the beeches towered and from which a long bushy ride thrust down through woodland. We stood together gazing fully at the house.

'It's certainly an attractive place,' I said happily, 'and wonderful country. The rookery's just right, too.'

'Big, though,' Martin said with his faintly melancholy realism. 'There'll be a damned lot of work to be done to keep it running.'

'Listen, everybody,' Anna was calling. 'We're going to tour the house systematically. Elaine and I have been over it already as you know, so we're going to take a party each. Let's start now because there's a great deal to do.'

The wind-blown February sunshine lit the estate in an erratic, ragged way that may have either harmonized with or propagated my moods. Slatey skeins of clouds swished like wild geese across the sun, making the woods and bare gardens wintry stark, and then it all seemed hopeless, unattainable. Then the geese-clouds passed and the sun propelled down, hot and brilliant, bringing an instant transportation of spring brightness to the country and to me: of course it was possible! Determination and imaginative financial juggling could make it possible.

We straggled through the stable yard, peeping into the silent cobwebby buildings, past the kitchen wing, and the small square lawn where I saw a nuthatch in the walnut tree beside the badminton hall, through the orchard of crooked, worn-out trees, and along the side of the wood. From there one's gaze went skimming like a partridge down the full-breasted bulge of park-like meadow, across a deep wooded gulley, and then on over a succession of high-hedged fields across the Gedd Valley to the distant rising mass of Ashcroft Park. We followed the boundary fence along the edge of the Park Field. The wind buffetted, first greyly cold, then charged with sunlight. My leg was beginning to ache sorely but I didn't care. This was an exploration into new country to be colonized.

There was an area of shrubbery and deliberately contorted lanes of Japanese cherries that made sudden secret twists, and a deep block of bushes in which I saw a jay's nest. Here was a derelict tennis court, invaded by thistles from which a family party of goldfinches flew, and standing near the gardener's house was a set of farm buildings, cowsheds and barns, with a tiny ruined cottage whose daub and wattle had gone to crumbs at one end. Then the kitchen garden, still serenely stylized with its ladders of fruit trees lining the tall, dark brick walls, and the copse behind which held a small annexe rookery.

It was a limited tour, confined to the perimeter of the house. As we circled it my eyes trailed desiringly over the fields and woods and thickets visible, wishing there was time to see what they held. Especially enticing was the expanse of commonland behind the house, islets of thorn and furze in washing seas of coppery bracken, that was enclosed by a ribbon of woodland – it would be a wonderful spring home for birds, linnets, of course, and perhaps shrikes and nightjars. When Andrew was older he and I would camp out there in a wigwam made of branches and bracken . . .

But there was no time then for tracing and siting airy plans for a dubious future. The financial gristle had to be chewed and, we hoped, digested. By two o'clock we were all sitting around a fire of fallen wood lit by Julian in the great open fireplace of the panelled hall. It was all very pleasant to know that everyone liked the place, was delighted with it, thought it the perfect setting for the experiment; but for Bee and me enchantment gradually dimmed when discussion began on the realities of money needed. How much could we contribute as capital investment? Nothing. How much could we pay as a weekly rate? Less than the lowest figure on the provisional scale of charges, assessed on the spot for the varying standards of accommodation that the house contained. We both sat silent in our corner seats in the train going home. Tired and dejected, neither of us was brave enough to say what was blatantly obvious: 'We can't do it.' We kept clear of the subject. After supper I was wiping while Bee washed the crockery, and I heard a tawny owl cry from the plane trees at the foot of the garden. Stupid owl, I thought, don't you know any better than to spend your few years of life in London, living on rubbish-dump rats and sooty little house sparrows? The long trembling hoot increased my depression and I spoke out: 'Well, it means taking the paper job, darling.'

Bee rubbed a saucepan an unnecessarily long time. 'Yes, I suppose it does mean that.'

I went to the bureau, intricately carved by a Flemish craftsman of the eighteenth century – it was one of the few pieces of our beachcombed furniture that I liked – and sadly typed the letter of acceptance of the newspaper job.

Chapter Two

The next two years was a period that mixed oddly happiness and unhappiness. In many ways I enjoyed my work on the paper, at first. A taste for criticism and a mild interest in the theatre found combined expression, and during that time I reviewed hundreds of plays, amateur and professional. On my entertainment page I also wrote up next week's films. If I had not had opportunity of seeing the films, I printed composite summaries of the opinions of critics whom I held in high regard, Lejeune, Dilys Powell and Richard Winnington. The results were high in the brow for our readership, but, despite the bellicose protests of local cinema managers, who resented the implication that any film being exhibited by them was not a world-beater, these and my dramatic notices gradually earned a reputation of dependability. I was also writing a weekly commentary, editorials, a countryside diary, and editing the gossip column. I escaped almost all the deadening routine reporting of local journalism, and I found it pleasant and invigorating again to see my name over articles and front-page 'lead' news stories.

Bee and I were living three miles out of town in a place called Horsemoor Green. It was joined to the town by an umbilical cord of detached managerial-class houses, but although now only a suburb, it retained some of its village atmosphere. Around the sixteenth-century church were a cluster of almshouses, picturesque, damp and cramped, flanked by the almost equally old Bull Inn. There was a village pond, too, an archipelago of tea-coloured water with islands of tins and bicycle parts, which from a distance added to the threadbare rural atmosphere. Now I had a car. When I first saw it it was drab in flaky grey paint, embossed with the heraldic symbols of military units. The sand of the Western Desert choked its overworked engine. But resprayed a glossy maroon, overhauled and tuned, I delighted to send it snorting down the curling Buckinghamshire lanes, hood down and windscreen flattened across the bonnet, increasing speed with quick twists of the motor-cycle hand throttle that surmounted the handicap of a tin leg.

It could have been a happy period but for the poison that seeped into personal relationships, both inside and outside the office, and the growth of a situation that impinged upon our marriage. I saw the baby weekly becoming thinner because of the tension, passed on to him by the atmosphere in which Bee and I lived, which prevented him from taking his food. In a moment of desperation I decided that the only remedy was to slash myself free from the office, and I left to work on an evening paper sixty miles away. I found some secret consolation in the knowledge that it was the paper for which Richard Jefferies, whose books had been dear to me, had worked as a youth. But the fact that Jefferies had walked the same streets, had crouched over his notebook in the same courtroom and council chamber, was not enough to sustain me. As I dragged through the bitter, iron, snow-blinded days of that awful January, I became more and more rawly exposed to the spirit that had killed the visionary farmer's son, the spirit of this town which was a monument to nineteenth-century industrialism, a town of railways and smoke and wastes of black slums. I did not stay long. There followed a frustrating period in publicity, in disseminating half-baked propaganda dollopped with artificial cream for a Government information department, where one's main stream of energy was expended in building up the reputation and ego of executives whose personalities and abilities were about equal in worth. Then, as if all the time it had been inevitable, as if all my intervening activities had been evasions, to Fleet Street.

I had been reporting for the Sunday paper for some weeks before the obvious suddenly struck me. Violet, our girl baby-sitter, had been put on sentry duty over Andrew, and Bee and I had driven to a nearby village for an evening drink. It was a trip we liked making. The drive was through the orchardland of Love Hill – where the post-horn pealing of wrynecks still sounded in spring – and through the surging summer greenness of the rolling hills to the quiet little village set between common and parkland. Bee, who was eight months pregnant, was sipping a mild ale and we sat on a bench while house martins swung chattering up to their nests under the 8-foot-high eaves. It was soothingly peaceful in the evening sun and the thought of returning to the shut-in atmosphere of our block of flats intruded distastefully. Opposite was a delightful house, white-painted with sunset-coloured roses clawing up the walls. The door, with its brass horseshoe knocker, was open, allowing a glimpse of a quarry-tiled hall, wheel-back chairs, and an Anne drop-leaf table.

'My god,' I sighed, 'wouldn't it be nice to be living somewhere like that?'

Bee made a sad sound of agreement. 'Just for the want of a few hundred pounds for a deposit.'

'I'd like to get right away from this area. But the only thing we could possibly buy would be a semi-detached villa. I'd as soon live in Hammersmith or Finsbury Park as sit like a trespasser in the middle of a field in a row of new little red houses. I wish I could think of something.'

We both stared at each other without speaking for a moment. And the instant I said 'Bereworde!' Bee followed with: 'That's just what I was going to say!'

'Of course,' I said excitedly. 'Why didn't we think about it before? There's nothing to hold us to this place now. And we could probably do it financially.' I swallowed my beer. 'Come on, we'll ring Anna tonight.'

On the way home Bee was less sure than I. That was to be expected. My progression through life was in a series of spurts, jumping from one impulse to another like a man leaping river boulders, a confused mixture of recklessness and hesitancy. When something alluring presented itself I attacked. If it was a book I wanted I spent my last ten shillings on it; if it was a job that gave me satisfaction I worked on it until I had drained myself hollow of vitality. Since I had walked out of the feature job we had regained most of our earlier happiness with each other, but complete stability was not yet established; we were still busy shoring up our marriage with trust and true companionship. Bee was doubtful. She was not sure that, at this point, it would be wise to go into the community and an atmosphere that might have an eroding effect on our family self-containment. I had no fears on this score. I was certain of us, but I was equally certain that I had to find a new base, new territory.

For in the past few months a wonderful thing had happened. I had had two books accepted by a publisher. The first was a collection of four bird and animal stories. Two had been written during a leave from the RAF which Bee and I spent in a caravan on the edge of a Sussex forest. It was autumn and it did not stop raining the whole week. After the first day we stopped bothering about trying to keep dry. We tramped through the streaming woodland collecting blackberries and hazel-nuts, and we cooked sausages on a hissing, smouldering fire. And in the evening by candlelight I wrote enjoyingly and without thought of publication, the stories of Whitestar the stoat and Smirril the hobby hawk. The other two were written in hospital between operations, escaping from the lonely chumminess of ward-life into the enchanted sunshine of boyhood.

The four stories added to a rubbish dump of miscellaneous manuscripts in the bottom drawer of the bureau. Later they were salvaged and sent, without any definite hopes, to a literary agent recommended to me by a good newspaper friend who had sold short stories for fantastic sums to *Colliers* and the *Saturday Evening Post*. Six months later had come the dramatic news that a publisher had agreed to publish them in book form. Lifted buoyantly into a realm where all things now seemed possible, I had returned to a novel abortively begun earlier, a novel about one of Britain's rarest birds, the little ringed plover, which I had watched in gravel pits in the district. Writing nightly into the early hours, working at a high emotional pressure, I finished it in two and a half months, and that was also accepted. It was to be published first, before the stories; in the following spring. The miracle had happened. I was an author and the future was golden. Now we had to live somewhere else where there was room for my expansion and where there was material that I needed.

We got home at ten and rang Anna immediately. It was some time before she could be found. Pips sounded with expensive persistence. There was some social chit-chat and then I put the question to her.

'Well, yes, as a matter of fact there is room for another family,' she said. 'Peter and Sally Andrews left last week. He's got a job in Jamaica. Look, could you come down for a weekend? You'll have to be looked over, you know. One of our few rules.'

The rule was observed the next weekend. It was a pleasant two days, drinking coffee and talking in the families' sitting rooms, before-breakfast strolls through the grounds, joining in the communal work. As was the custom, we spent some time in the company of all the families, for each to assess their personal feelings towards us (and for us to do the same towards them) and our potential value as members of the community. Four days after returning to the flat we had a letter from Anna. At the previous evening's family meeting a vote had been taken on our application. There had been general agreement that we should take up residence at Bereworde.

Now that the decision was known the attitudes held by Bee and me took sudden and extreme swings. Her doubts vanished. She was enthusiastic, chiefly for Andrew's sake, I think. He was now nearly two years old and his sensitive, emotional temperament had suffered from flat life. Not to have outlet to anywhere but a tiny paved courtyard was bad enough, but far more harmful had been our constant checkings to prevent the bad-tempered broomstick thumping and shouted protests that came from the flat below if ever he ran across the floor or banged a toy. Bee had seen him during that weekend gazing with timid wonder at the vastness of lawns and fields, and she had seen the happily-grubby Bereworde children climbing trees, riding the swings and yelling in the sandpit. If there had been no other reason she would have gone there only to see Andrew given the chance to develop freely and happily. But there were other reasons also.

'You've no idea, darling, how stimulating it was to be able to talk to other women about things besides rations and clothes and cooking,' she said. 'It's not so bad for you. You're out every day meeting new people and seeing new things. But since we left London I feel as if my brain has mummified.'

I knew how she felt. At Horsemoor Green we had made friends, four or five young couples whom we saw around the village and who usually came down to the White Horse for a Saturday-night drink. They were likable but their interests were narrow. No, I would have no regrets at leaving Horsemoor Green. Apart from the stifling character of flat-life, there were too many bad memories rooted in the phase that was ending. On the other hand, the Bereworde weekend had set doubts sprouting like thistles. I liked the people, most of them, and the place still glowed with the radiance of an ideal, but was the transition going to be made smoothly? Life would be of a very different pattern. I was not sure that I was sufficiently flexible to adapt myself boldly. The war, the leg, the intellectual scene — too many adjustments had had to be made this past few years; one was an ill-finished unit composed of badly-fitting parts. I was no longer sure about it, but nor were my doubts clear enough to provide basis for any opposition. We confirmed that we would be coming but not until September. Notice had to be given at the flat and Bee was booked at the hospital for her baby. September would be the time, and I sent two pounds to Ruthene Hobson, who did the community odd-jobbing, asking her to give the two top-floor rooms a new coat of paint.

Chapter Three

This was the landscape, these were the figures.

Eight families were living in the house. Our suite was between the Harpers' and the Hobsons'. John Harper, who served as a Naval lieutenant on motor-torpedo boats with Peter Scott, had been in advertising before the war; unable to face the return to a world of vicious competitiveness and sharp minds, he had put all his gratuity into starting a photography business with Gerald Tarrant, Anna's elder brother. Their studio was in the stables and both wondered despondently at times if they had not backed the wrong race. He was a big, organ-voiced man with a heavy Orson Welles face and a vocabulary vivid with motor-torpedo boat adjectives. Hilary, small, dark, with a machine-gun vocal delivery, was his wife, and they had two children, Brenda, five, and Miff, two. They had been at Bereworde from the start.

Basil and Ruthene Hobson were later arrivals. They lived in the east-wing room, which seemed to have been built from bricks of books. Overloaded bookshelves encircled the room end-to-end. He was a farmer, and prospective MP for an Oxfordshire constituency. Somewhere down in Wiltshire he had a farm but he had come to Bereworde mainly for the utilitarian reason of being nearer his constituency. Small, swarthy, Lawrencian-bearded, he went rocking off most evenings in his senile car to distant political meetings. During the day he worked for the Bereworde horticultural society. Ruthene was tall and achieved a bohemian elegance in multi-patched slacks and gaudy neckerchiefs. She wrote a little, occasionally submitting a short story for a Third Programme competition. Her eight-year-old son Sebastian, the eldest Bereworde child, once, when asked why he wouldn't join in a game with the younger children, announced: 'I don't find that sort of thing very amusing. My interests are Art, Music and Literature.' Sitting with touselled hair and grubby knees, he read Lucretious on *The Nature of Things* over the teatable. Four-year-old Rolfe was his brother.

Also on our floor lived Terry, who had left school only a few months ago and come to join the John–Gerald studio. Daughter of the chief of a BBC region, she took lovely, sensitive photographs of children. She was not officially a member of the community but lived as one. Below were the Parfitts and next to them Alec and Flora Cameron, a Scots couple with two children. They were both Marxists but inactive politically. He worked for a firm of publishers and Flora, who was an Edinburgh University MA, ran a vague nursery class for the younger children, whose function was chiefly to take them off their mothers' hands for a couple of hours in the morning.

Further down the corridor were the Barlows, the previous arrivals to ourselves, who had not long been married. Christopher was a lean, languid pleasant man with a stammer, a doctor working in a hospital research laboratory, whose appearance gave no clue to his extreme left political views and his war record as a red-bearded Commando major. He painted in a delicate Impressionistic style in the derelict tennis court pavilion. His wife, Harry, had been a very young ward sister who was working at the hospital where he went after demobilization. She did her job as Bereworde's housekeeper with dynamic efficiency, not lessened by the fact that she was pregnant.

Representing yet another life-attitude were the Morrises, a Catholic family. Aubrey was a middle-aged barrister who hovered around the Labour Party right wing and who took his responsibilities as a member of the community with profound seriousness. Gladys had been a schoolteacher and still retained a strong redolence of University blue-stocking days. They had three daughters.

On the ground floor were Jim and Mary Stubbs; Jim, the eldest member of the community, was a cheery, joke-cracking 50-year-old Cockney, manager of a small engineering factory, the friendliest, most mild-mannered, least aggressive Communist that could be imagined. Poor Mary, who was not well even then, died a year later. They had no children.

Living in the cottage adjoining the house was Mrs Baxter, a remarkable old lady of eighty-five. She was tiny and frail-looking as an anaemic child, and had the vitality of a steer. Every day she worked in the kitchen gardens and in the middle of winter walked the eight miles to Downsteeple and back across the fields. Nor was she a member of the community, but unlike Terry she took no part in it beyond displaying a grandmotherly interest in its well-being. She was the mother of an ex-member and had stayed on after her daughter had left.

In the lodge were living the Sullivans, Ham and Margit, and their three little girls. He was an American novelist. They had come to England on a scholarship. He was an angular, dark man of dark, thin moods, and since he had been at Bereworde he had tried writing in the house, in the ruined cottage, in a room at the gardener's cottage, and in a stable loft. After several months he and his pretty Hungarian wife, who had been a concert violinist, moved into the lodge. Still he appeared to find it difficult to write.

The only other apartment in regular use was Julian's stable room. He was now working as assistant film director for a London documentary company and came down only at weekends. By the time we arrived Martin and Elaine Larkin had left, as had two or three other families, for reasons which ranged from inability to endure the daily journey to London to a battle-clash of temperaments.

Bereworde was blessed with many bathrooms. It worked out to one for each family. Each family had two rooms, a nursery bedroom for the children and a bed-sitting room for the parents. The rooms varied in size, attractiveness and price. The top floor, where we were to live, had been the servants' quarters in the manor's more spacious days. Those who lived on the first floor paid more for their larger, lighter quarters. The adults ate communally in the oak room, once the library. There was a long, curved table and also several smaller ones. It was a pleasant room, panelled to the ceiling in dark oak, with a great stone arched fireplace and deep windows facing on to the terrace and the stepped lawns that led down to the Park Field. The children had their own communal dining-room in the kitchen corridor, so that there was the quiet of segregation at meal times. The families furnished their own rooms and contributed any surplus furniture to the communal rooms.

Almost all the men worked in London during the week and were expected to put in a minimum of five hours' communal work which could be spread out as preferred over evenings and the weekend. For the women, who were in occupation all the time, there was a household rota, which in theory fairly distributed all the domestic tasks extra to looking after individual suites. The staff consisted of a cook and her handyman husband, and a kitchen maid.

We moved in on a Friday. Rain sluiced down steadily from a dour autumn sky and a mud-trail wound up the two long flights of stairs. For the Bereworde children it was an exciting event and for several hours the tramp of boots, the crash of furniture against bannisters and doorposts, and the gleeful screams of children rang through the house. Yet by tea-time we were fairly well organized. I stood blinking tiredly through cigarette smoke at the room. It looked attractive. The room was conveniently divided by a cupboard unit that jutted from the doorway a third of the way into the floor space. In the recess had gone the divan and dressing table. Opposite them, under the window, was my desk. The other half was the living part. Bookshelves slotted neatly into the matching recess. There were beams across the ceiling, and the dormer windows, set deeply into the sloping roof, were framed with thick tresses of creeper. The view was magnificent, a rook's view right across the dipping fields and the valley to the distant hill-line; and not a building, not even a farm.

Baby Amanda was oblivious to her new surroundings but Andrew was late going to sleep that night. When we had had supper I went into his room and for a while we sat at the window looking out into the dusk. We were almost level with the rooks' nests. The heavy foliage of the beeches was beginning to fray and the black splotches could be picked out, but there were no birds there now; on this night they were not even roosting at their colony.

'Are you going to like it here, Roo?' I said softly as he curled up warmly in my arms.

'Yes, I am,' he said firmly. Already that evening he had been out to explore the sand-pit and try out some of the toys lying about. Big-eyed and staring out on to the dim crescent of sward far below from which the beeches rose like smooth marble pillars. 'Can't we see a long way, daddy!' Until now his view had been halted by roofs a few yards away.

'When spring comes you'll be able to sit here and watch the rooks building their nests. You'll like that won't you, Roo?'

'Yes, me will. And, daddy – will the rooks have eggs?'

He loved birds. At a year old he used to sit fascinated on the kitchen table in the flat watching the robin and the chaffinches and, sometimes, a pied wagtail that came on to the low roof outside to peck at the crusts we threw out. Now there would be no need for him to crouch with nose pressed to a window pane. He could run and sit among them. 'Tomorrow,' I said, 'we'll see if we can see any rabbits, shall we?'

'Oh, yes!' he shouted. He threw himself on to his bed and rolled into the blankets. Seconds later he was asleep. Bee was still unpacking suitcases and filling drawers. She was moving slower and slower. 'Come on, let's forget all the rest now. Anna asked us to have coffee.'

Instead of going to bed early as we had intended we sat up until past one o'clock talking and drinking coffee that got progressively blacker and bitterer each time it was re-heated. I was prickly-eyed with weariness but I was enjoying it all too much to break away. It was exhilarating to be sitting around a spluttering wood fire in the warmth and security of a circle of new friends, while the rain *shrrd* against the panes and the wind made the trees groan. People came and went. Gerald arrived with Bill Carr-Forbes and another of his friends from the village, both in caps and duffel coats, for they drove fierce-looking sports cars (one an Alvis and the other a one-and-a-half litre TT replica Frazer Nash). Flora stayed for a while, and Ham Sullivan came to demand, truculently, an increase in his coal ration and stayed for two hours talking about Pound's *Piza Cantos*. Julian was there, for he had arrived that evening from London, with him an Indian woman who worked for the same film unit.

The company, the civilized talk, getting to know interesting new people – yes, it was all enjoyable. Yet before long I was going to find that, for me, this very enjoyment was one of the essential dangers of Bereworde. Always there were too many diversions, always there was an excellent reason for not shutting oneself away and working, and always if one *did* isolate oneself behind a locked door, there was the nagging guilty feeling that it was a desertion of one's community duties.

That night the conversation was mostly about children and their upbringing. It was a joy to us, and to Bee particularly, to discover that all of our half-formulated, instinctively-felt ideas were in line with the general Bereworde attitude. I say general because, although there was an agreement on broad principles, there was a wide range of opinions that by no means always harmonized. Anna stood for the most positive – or negative – form of freedom. She was a Reichian and her eldest daughter was soon going to a Neillian boarding school. She emphatically rejected parental discipline, in even its subtlest, mildest form. Self-regulation was her creed, which rested on the belief that the child was the best judge of its needs, and that a fully developed personality could be achieved only without adult moulding and forcing. I found myself arguing back on many points, yet it was in a spirit of questioning rather than opposition. And even if I could not loyally follow the Reichian theories into their farthest reaches, at least it was a language I understood and was in tune with. Since before we had had Andrew I had known that the treatment a child received from its first living moments was of supreme importance. I had read none of A.S. Neill's books, I had only vaguely heard of Homer Lane and Madame Montessori. Reich, I had never heard of at all. Yet on every side, wherever there were parents and children, I saw distortion of child characters being carried out, more frustrated, unhappy people being made. It cut right through society, from the sleep-cheated whining youngsters playing lethargically in city streets until supper of fish and chips and late night radio dance music, to the sterilized, correctly behaved upper-middle-class child, disciplined by caste dogma, his natural self 'don'ted' out of existence. Those were the roots of a neurotic modern world and it was there that reform had to start, with the baby, that was obvious. But in our previous surroundings any attempt to put those beliefs into words was received with the incomprehension that might have been the response to a speech in a Malayan dialect. My editor, just before Andrew was born, had given me advice on how to rear children. 'Just like you train a dog,' he explained. 'They've got to be drilled, taught to come to heel when you say so.' His son, who never got dirty, who recited conventional politenesses to visitors, suddenly at the age of five began bed-wetting to the chagrined bewilderment of his parents. A young and likeable woman in our flats considered Bee cranky because she quoted a statement of Susan Isaacs, most moderate and restrained of the early child psychologists.

So it was a liberation to sit and talk about these things to people who had the same terms of reference. But another thing that we were to discover before long was that, even in this civilized atmosphere, where even the most cautious rejected corporal punishment as a barbarity, there could be bad collisions between different brands of 'advanced' outlooks.

We went to bed happy that night. There was no sound from the cardboard horn above our bed that relayed through a gramophone soundbox any restlessness from the children's room. I slept as soundly as they and did not wake until the clanging breakfast bell roused me to the streaming sunshine of a lovely September day.

Chapter Four

There was a kitchen crisis. The cook had walked out. From the talk over the breakfast table I gathered that it was the climax to an extended subdued war between the cook and her husband on one side and Harry and the Berewordean women on the other. They were discussing it with a certain solemnity, which was understandable since it would mean cooking going on the rota until a new cook was found.

I was not especially interested. I was eager to get outside and enter into the day's activities. Only Christopher Barlow had gone into business. The other men were in exceptionally old old clothes. John, in crimson shirt and blue corduroys with a rent in the seat, said: 'Logging this morning, Ken?'

'Yes, I'd like to.'

'Good. That makes three of us to start with and there'll be more along later. There's a tree to get down on Clementine Farm. I don't think it'll be much trouble. I suggest we get started right away.'

The farmer wanted to rid his field of the cherry stump; the community wanted wood for the winter. It was a fair deal, and the three of us, John, Julian and myself, set off along the lane with long-handled axes, cross-saw, beetle, wedges, sledge hammer and a rope with a breaking strain of two-and-a-quarter tons. My muscles felt eagerly tensed, ready to sweat away the accumulated mental dust of a week in Fleet Street.

The Michaelmas sun was warm on the skin and the edges of the oak, elm and beech leaves were stained as if from dabbling in its rosiness. A robin was fluting with loud nostalgia in the hedge. It did not stop as we passed close, continuing to point its beak skyward and squeeze out the long rich whistles. It was standing on a rose sprig hung with the shiny scarlet globules and the instant impression was of glutinous beads of blood escaping from its raw breast.

Some jackdaws went overhead towards the house yapping like puppies. The early mist, which had smelt of mushrooms and dying insects when I first left the house, had been heated away by the sun, and now there was an illusion of summer. But the air was very still, autumnly ruminative, and the ragged *clack clack* of iron on iron sounded with ringing clearness from where Basil was splitting logs in the chestnut drive beyond the left-hand hedge.

Crossing the field to the stump, I began to have a secret regret that it was to be thrown, for I was thinking of the kestrels and owls that must have lived there. It was an old tree. It stood alone in the centre of the meadow, a gnarled finger with a broken brown nail. We dropped the tackle on the grass near a stub of wood, half-submerged in bramble and nettle, that had snapped from the top, and walked around the tree prospectively, seeing where the blades and teeth could best bite.

From the base, where it was thicker than our three bodies together, to the shattered spire, it reached a full twenty feet. But for a single ricketty branch that thrust out suppliantly, and which sucked up enough life to nourish a threadbare shawl of fine-toothed leaves, the trunk was naked. It must have been a fine, brawny tree at its full height, before the superstructure of boughs, with their bunches of pallid-pink blossom, died and fell away, leaving only the grooved and pocked pillar.

It was rotten at the heart. Three or four holes gaped in the horny bark where branches had dropped from their sockets. There, the wood was brown as congealed blood, foxy in woodman's language. The stump looked bound to stagger back before the first powerful wind and fall. Surely, the slicing blows of the axes, the drive of the saw would be even more devastatingly decisive?

That line of thought was jerked to a stop by the discovery of a wound unlike the branch cavities. On the flank a few feet above ground there was a criss-cross pattern of scars. Evidently someone else had been here with a similar idea. That person's axe had gashed the tree about, had clawed out a patch of bark so that the underlying pinkness was exposed, but had got not much deeper. There was exhaustion and loss of direction written in those rough jags. The axe had been leaned on, the tree glared at, then the person had rummaged around in the grass for kindling that the wind had felled . . .

Well, the stump might be tougher than it looked, but our approach to the job was not in the half-hearted spirit of our predecessor. Nor did we intend to waste that solid weight of wood bunched in the base by cutting three feet from the ground. We were claiming it all.

There were two main root spurs, each a solid buttress formed by an ankylose growth of perhaps half a dozen root stems, anchoring the stump hard. These should be the first to be cut, thus severing the cherry's last complete hold. John began with the axe, making downward inward-slanting drop blows that sent sharp, hard little chips shooting through the air. One struck me on the arm and it stung like a flint. I picked it up and fingered it. It was fibrous and hard, sapless, the salmon-pink wood ossified into strong, deep grains, made by the surge of crude fluid from the roots to the leaf refineries – for how many years? I wondered.

It was my turn with the axe. I straddled in John's stance, feeling the weight and the subtle balance of the axe-head on its glass-smooth swans-neck elm helve, then letting it glide up with the soft impetus of its own weight. It thudded down, clipping deeply into the ruddled pit made by John, and to free it I had to chuck the handle thrice. It was good to feel the axe's dynamic mass, first hanging slack-headed during the over-shoulder swing, then flying forward, suddenly a living force, jumping down and into the wood with an iron exclamation. . . . It was good until the arms and wrists missed the cue from the brain, or the eye guide-line to the right nick got ravelled, and the axe skidded on to the wood like a sparrow-hawk botching a strike. Then the blade bounced back with a flat grunt and the vibrations ran through the handle like an electric shock, leaving the bones in the palms numb and aching.

By the time the two main spurs had been cut we were all looking more serious. This was going to be no push-over, in any sense. John and Julian took the cross-saw and poised it low on the bole. After a few stuttering shunting motions, the teeth began to slice and the blade became a piston of dull blue light. I sat on the end of the fallen top-knot, where it protruded from the blackberry bush, and watched the break-up of the social systems that had evolved within the hide of the cherry.

The woodlice were out first and then I watched a brindled spider with hooked hairy legs come scuttling from under a ridge of bark. It stopped, sidled on an inch, then squatted on a wart-like excrescence while its thick capsular body dithered to the rhythm of the saw. The woodlice wove around the spider, blindly and helplessly scurrying up one groove and down the next. The spider sat stilly, meditatively, while the orange wood-dust spurted about it, and the woodlice went on in their dizzy tour of despair. The spider looked stunned by the catastrophe. It made a tiny movement, an impulsive flicker of a leg. I saw that descending the stump, away from the widening pink grin where the saw was working in, was a dowdy insect with a stout, gross little body. It was this that the spider was watching. . . . The saw *harrhed* and *hurrhed* like a December gale, and the cherry quivered faintly. The tick laboriously fled down the escarpment of the collar, away from the roar and rattle of danger. The spider stockily waited.

For a doubtful moment I thought I was wrong, that the tick would pass safely. There was a swift kicking movement and the tick had disappeared beneath the spider's spread body. The whiskered legs carved. . . . The wood powder floated in soft puffs, and efficiently the spider parcelled up the tick, contemptuous, it seemed, of the break-up of its castle.

At that moment I felt a prick on my wrist and scrambling through the hairs, glossy as a blob of amber, was an ant. As I flicked it off I saw that the shimmer of ant bodies under the top-knot was like running resin. I was obviously causing consternation in the nest beneath the log.

I jumped up and began to chop and drag away the skeins of bramble with the pick. The top-knot could go as it was back to the house for splitting. I was glad to be moving again, for I had been getting cold. Mares'-tails – the wispy feather-like cirrus that means rain – were curling across the blue. The sun could still be seen, but it was now a dim taper behind the cloud. I was warm again after only a minute or two of prising and rolling the log on to clear grass, where it could be handled. I felt free and happy, intact, and I welcomed the aching drag in the muscles that told that they were being redrafted into use. This was communal life as I had imagined it at my most optimistic moments, working alongside one's friends in a spirit of complete harmony. Here, with the September air soft on the face and a part of a flow of unity and happiness, I felt that the experiment must be a success. It had in it the essence of the good co-operative life that man could live, but would not.

By the time Ian arrived the cherry had been undercut. The two claws were snipped and the saw had made a circular incision around the collar. The theory was that with a rope slung about the top, the rest would merely be a matter of concentrated weight. John climbed up and draped the rope around the trunk. We were dubious. Might not the stump be beheaded at the first jerk, leaving the bulk standing firm? But that was the best angle of leverage, so the risk must be taken. The rope was stretched to a heavily-crowned elm, a mature and majestic tree, about thirty yards away, so that it was at fingertip height.

At a shouted signal everyone, with Brenda tugging frenziedly at John's trousers, threw themselves upon the rope. The rope swivelled about, jerking in abrupt little arcs, but the cherry barely budged. The rope was tightened. We all jumped on again. After five minutes Brenda wandered off. After another tighten and pull the rope was abandoned, and everyone walked up to the cherry. There was much peering and poking and discussion. The saw began rasping once more.

I sat where I had fallen from the rope, wondering what was keeping the stump up. It looked rotten as soddened cork; it was hollow; the tough rind had been almost completely cut through; it shook and grunted at each tug. And it didn't come down. With a noise like a tin of stones a magpie hopped the lane hedge and, followed by two more, wavered across the field. That made eleven I had seen since breakfast within a few hundred yards of the house. And not long ago the magpie had been almost extinct in this border country of Bedfordshire, Buckinghamshire and Hertfordshire, I had been told. Now chequered wings and tails like trailing swords were an everyday sight.

I must get a young magpie for Andrew next year. . . . I began thinking of the good things there would be to do in the spring – so many things, alluring across the grey plain of winter. But at close quarters would they seem less important than a dozen other matters clamouring for attention? Would they be postponed and dodged, so that another spring would have passed, and, in the aridity of an August day, I would suddenly be poignantly conscious of the wasted months behind, and of other lost springs when writing seemed more urgent than the sunsparkle upon new leaves? That was how it seemed always to have been in the past; but here, I felt, all that would change. Here I could find that balanced happiness I wanted.

A shout from John cut off my thoughts. I walked over, rubbing away a damp spot that had spread upon my seat. The form was this, Julian explained: the saw would cut no deeper. The stump was still gripping tenaciously with roots that could not be reached and was sitting hard on the inner rim. Its hold, however, had been loosened still more, so first we'd have another swing on the rope. If that didn't work, well, a tractor was the next line of attack.

We marshalled ourselves in a straggling line while Julian again tightened the rope. With less vigour than before we threw on our combined weight. This time the cherry rocked, slightly but perceptibly. It rocked, but stubbornly it stood.

No more time was wasted. John strode off to the farmhouse. I shared a cigarette with Christopher and then we began to load the top-knot and other scattered chunks on to the handcart that had been brought up. The 26-inch automatic saw could cope with the log as it was. We had just got it balanced properly when Alf, the farmer's son, drove the tractor through the gate.

It was a cheering sight as it came throbbing across the field with the last peaky rays of the swamped sun gleaming on the blue engine cowling. The rope was freed from the elm and the tractor's tow-pin dropped through its looped end. In first gear John eased forward until the rope was taut. There was a moment's pause in which the chant of a coal tit could be heard, then the throttle opened and the tractor set itself against the strain. For a second it seemed to hesitate while the engine hammered; there was a growl and a shudder from the stump; and the rope snapped and coiled back like a striking snake.

This time it was given a triple turn around the trunk and the tractor moved off taking up the slack in another direction to test for weakness. Again it edged forward while the rope stretched tremulously. The engine throbbed and roared, and the big steel-lugged wheels jerked round in inches. There was a second when it seemed that anything might happen, then movement of stump, rope and tractor was suspended. Then the stump gave a lurch, the ground around it heaved, and with a slow, grinding, splintering groan it heeled over upon its side.

We gathered around. It had broken off low, at ground level, but on one side it had dragged out its roots with it, long stiff tentacles that dripped damp mould. The cross-sawing had helped considerably. It was there that the trunk had surrendered. Long gouts of the rocky-looking red wood had been torn out from the stem and smaller sharp spars bristled around the gape. The stump had been lain low and now the real job was beginning, the cutting.

After lunch rain started. It fell finely, thinly, and a robin, perhaps the same robin, sang sadly in the thorn clump. Yet it was warm and soon we took off our coats and worked with our shirts pasted damply to our shoulders. Only John and I turned up in the afternoon. First we snedded away the single living bough and then we cross-sawed. We sat either side of the trunk and were soon working to a steady rhythm, feeling through the sliding saw the shift of weight and the pull of the other's body. But the saw would not go through. When the top was down to bark level it began to jam and stall, before it was deep enough to pin in a wedge above it.

We axed and sawed again. The stump was hard to work, lacking the pliant submissiveness of living wood, and cutting was tiring. The teeth grated against the tough fibres as if against seams of concrete and the blade was not oiled by sap. While we cut I wondered how long the erosion of wind and rain, and the dynamiting effect of frost, would have taken to demolish the cherry. How many winters would it have needed to crack that iron structure? How long had it taken to wear it down to its present state? The longer we sawed, the more remote seemed the answers.

At last the tangled hinges of the roots were severed and the battered top cut off. There was left the long horny barrel of the main trunk, too wide, too grizzled, too contorted with knots for the saw. We began to split. The first wedge was poised at the top in the very centre of the trunk where the bark had flaked, and made firm with a few taps from the sledge. At each heavy blow the wedge jerked in another fraction, until half its length was buried in the reluctantly-yielding wood. Another, with a broken head, was jammed to the side of the first wedge, and knocked level, then a third. And the three, making a single wide wedge, were driven down, with a persistence that at first seemed unequal to the rigid resistance of the wood, but after a score of blows they sank with quickly increasing depth into a crooked crimson vein that began to wriggle down the trunk.

Now each fresh plunge of the sledge was widening the gap. More wedges were thrust in at intervals and hammered until their heads were flush. And each blow was now followed by a sullen crackle that continued for a few seconds after the wedge had been struck, a creaking and a groaning from the heart of the trunk that was sweet to the ears. The cherry was breaking.

The end came with a loud crunching report and softly the trunk sagged open. A kick, and it fell wide apart, revealing the torn, ragged core of the tree, red within as a human limb but for a long hollow where the wood was a dark colour. This was the chamber to which the branch-sockets had led and it held a mess of short black twigs, the remnants of a jackdaw's nest.

We stood back, leaning on hammer and axe, and looked at the dismembered tree, at the shambles of trampled bramble and nettle around it, and at the thickly scattered debris, the chips and hanks of pink wood that littered the grass. Then I saw within the raw cavern something stuck upright upon a little rough shelf. I stepped closer and saw that what for a moment I had thought to be a dead leaf was a sleeping butterfly. Its wings were closed above its body, showing only the drab brown undersurfaces, held flatly tight as hands in prayer, and it did not move when I touched it with my finger.

I dislodged it and bore it upward in the palm of my hand. Still it slept in the deep unconsciousness of hibernation. I blew upon it gently, then harder and after a few seconds its wings fluttered vaguely, showing the brilliant whorls of colour that mark the peacock.

For a while it sat in my hand, weakly flickering those glowing wings, then abruptly fluttered up. Briefly it flew, aimlessly, dazedly, until suddenly an agitation and strength entered its flight, and it began to fly in quick, tumbling circles like a lapwing about its invaded territory. It drew a wavering fiery trail about the felled cherry – a flimsy living segment broken from the deadness of the tree. For nearly four minutes it flew in this way; then it branched away and, climbing steeply, was lost from sight in the greyish auburn-flecked greenness of the elm's top branches.

We turned away and in the rapidly fading light began loading the handcart for the last journey back to the house.

Chapter Five

At first it was like making probing explorations from an advance camp. I wanted to know familiarly the country I was living in. Estodham village was the highest in the county, but that was below the house, a mile away in a basin rimmed by gorse-brilliant common. Bereworde was perched seven hundred feet up on a rib of land, on successive layers of chalk marl, Totternhoe stone, hard chalk, Melbourn rock and flinty soft chalk that built up the Chiltern escarpment. To the north the country fell in slow undulations, an isolated region of farmland, tangled woods and narrow bushy lanes, until sliced across by the busy northbound traffic of Watling Street. Eastward were the downs, and the white road that swung along the great bluffs where winds battered through the hottest summer sun, and beneath was the vast mosaic that joined the Vale of Aylesbury. From the gates of Bereworde the lane rushed fast as a trout stream down the full green billows of Deadmanseye Hill to the valley where snipe and redshank nested in the reedy meadows beside the River Gedd. Beeches that formed towering woods and lined the steep-banked lanes with filigrees of exposed roots were the typical tree, but the wild cherry and the holly grew immense and prolific in the 'bottoms' and on the 'hoos', those spurs of land which gave the name to many of the farms and hills.

Records show that for centuries there had been a house on the site and the name, first mentioned in the Domesday Book in 1086, had probably meant the enclosure of Baere, the name of a family that in some early age had farmed the land. With Estodham (meaning homestead), Bereworde had until recent years been partly in Hertfordshire and partly in Bedfordshire, but had finally been given to Bedfordshire. The estate had been carved out of the Great Chiltern Forest and to these parts in Norman times royal and noble huntsmen had journeyed from London to hunt deer and boar. Many of the lanes had originally been marked out as pack-horse ways, while the wide grass verges that lined some of them showed that they had been cattle routes leading from the eastern counties.

But it was not until later that I struck out into the surrounds. First I wanted to look at the estate itself. On the map a thick crescent behind the rookery grove was marked as Estodham Common, but the thorn brakes, the foaming seas of bracken, the furze (it was here that poor villagers were allowed to cut 'fuzzen stalks' for fire lighting and heating ovens) had all gone. Now there was billiard table pasture. In the eyes of the War Agricultural Executive it had been wasteland. The bulldozers and ploughs had come, the nightjars and nightingales had fled. It was a disappointment, but there was too much else to see to worry unduly about that.

In any case there was a remnant left, a strip, 25-foot deep, of mixed fern and thorn, with an occasional gorse bush humped like a decorated hedgehog. A flock of siskins, greenish fork-tailed birds from Northern Europe, were often about there that winter, feeding in the birches. Alongside was a spinney of firs where pigeons roosted and where I often saw a tawny owl sleeping pressed tight against a slender black trunk. There was a warren and the rabbits made the bramble clumps quake with their bustle as you approached, and during daylight they slept out in the brushwood that had been heaped against the laneside hedge. Often I borrowed John's twelve-bore shotgun and wandered around here – rarely firing but enjoying the feeling of being able to bring in a rabbit for the communal pot now and again – and down the shrub-walled corridor of the ride, where I regularly saw a hunting cock sparrow-hawk.

October smeared a rosiness upon the field hedges of thorn, elder and wild rose, and bramblings fed with the chaffinch flocks. I saw great bands of lapwings stringing across the pigeon-grey skies and the winter parties of fieldfares and redwings were here, jerking eyes to themselves by their throaty cackles as they passed over. The leaves fell away from the beeches, leaving the rookery nests bare and black, and always there was the screeching of jays ripping out of the Long Wood.

Tits, so many of them, blue and great and coal, and the sober little marsh tit, were ever about the house; and on a frost-spangled morning I looked from the window to see a hare loping idly across the lawn. Across the Park Field was the Long Wood, a shadowy scrawl of trees. Still I had not visited it, and I wanted to because I knew that a month ago the Hertfordshire Hounds had found there and the Bereworde children had seen the fox running alongside the boundary fence. Also I wanted to go there because I had discovered that the Long Wood had a curious fame. Conchologists had elected it as the best place in the county for finding the beech-loving snail *cochlodina laminata*, while the even rarer snail, *acanthinula aculeata* had been found nowhere else in the county. I had no deep interest in snails and could not tell one type from another, but the wood's special characteristic (it seemed also to house an impressive variety of slugs) interested me. But still I had not gone there. I was beginning to find that escape from Bereworde and its duties and its attractions was not easily made.

I was sitting shivering while an electric fire scorched my shoe soles in the tiny top-floor room which I had started using. Working in our room had been impossible. People came in to talk; Bee wanted the radio on; and I found, too often, that I was more in the mood for talking or listening to the radio than for working. I moved typewriter, table and books next door. I liked the room. It was no more than four feet wide and painted a stark white. It had a satisfactory monastic asceticism about it; not even patterned wallpaper to distract. The door opened hesitantly but I did not look up. I was trying to start a book about an adventure of two boys with a snow leopard which they abducted from a downland zoo and took with them to live in a derelict estate called Bereworde.

'Wowk with daddy?' said the voice.

It had a note of cajoling anxiety in it, an edge of wistfulness. 'Daddy 'n' A-roo wowk?'

I turned round impatiently from the words that were pinned as dead as mounted butterflies on the paper. The smile was dubious, a little tremulous. 'Daddy 'n' A-roo wowk,' he repeated more firmly.

He was holding a Wellington boot in each hand. His eyes gazed apprehensively through the cluster of dark curls across his forehead. I gazed back silently, thinking how simple it must seem to Andrew: the sun was flattened against the frosted panes, making them little squares of tinfoil; the cry of a jackdaw on the roof came down the chimney into the room; here were the boots and the coat – all that had to be done was put them on, and the walk was started. And why not? I thrust the paper aside and jumped up.

'Of course we'll go for a walk, Andrew,' I said. 'Come on, boots on.'

Now that he had won, his independence returned. 'My do it,' he stated peremptorily, and with a volley of little grunts began to pull the boots on to the wrong feet.

We were outside in five minutes. The air was stingingly cold and Andrew's nose was like a cherry over his scarf. A nuthatch, a stubby blue-backed little bird, flew off the terrace as we walked out. It had been eating the red berries of the yew hedge. I had often watched it taking the berries on to a nearby ash, wedging them in a particular crevice and hammering it until it reached the kernel.

We walked slowly across the tussocky lower lawn towards the orchard, Andrew stepping high across the mounds of knotted stems, each one anointed with rime so that beneath the pale sun the grass was glimmer-shot. The orchard had been restocked with a dozen three-year-old Golden Gage plum trees. They looked healthy but it was doubtful if they would carry any crop for they had been waiting a fortnight out of soil before being planted. Most of the other trees were senile, bearded with grey-green lichen and rheumatically contorted. As we passed through the wooden gate, a green woodpecker gave its insane guffaw, so loudly and so near that it made me jump and caused Andrew to ask, 'What that funny noise, daddy?' We watched it vaulting away through the trees, its flight like the swift, soaring-skimming passage of a skier. Woodpeckers came often to the orchard, spiralling up the old twisted branches, testing the bark with short exploratory raps, snicking in insects with dabs of their rough-tipped tongues.

There were cows in the meadow. They were fine Jerseys, mulberry and dappled fawn and white, with the lean lines of good dairy stock. Stilly they watched us as we approached, watching us with their vague, beautiful eyes. It was difficult to get Andrew past. He loved cows with a passion he displayed towards no other animal. He had no fear of their size. He gambolled towards them, crooning 'Nice moonows, nice moonows' over and over again, smiling encouragingly and stretching his hand to stroke their enormous silky thighs.

It was difficult. I wanted him to be afraid of nothing, to have the capacity of direct and naturally flowing love towards life and all things that were life. Yet I was afraid that one day a cow, in a typical spasm of panic, would heave round and strike him with a hoof. I squatted beside him, near the first cow, which had not moved but stood staring bewilderedly with lowered head at Andrew's tiny smiling figure.

'Better not go any nearer, old chap,' I murmured, trying to explain. How could one teach caution without transplanting adult fear, that later would become a self-replenished reservoir of hatred, always ready to be directed at the person or thing that was feared? 'They're very big and clumsy animals, you see, and they might hurt Andrew without meaning to.'

'No, *nice* moonows,' he insisted indignantly, and the dreamy haze of love came back into his eyes as he stroked the air between him and the cow.

I attempted diversion by holding out a tuft of plucked grass. The cow wove its steaming wet nostrils several inches away from the extended grass but did not take it. Lumberingly, it backed away, and I drew Andrew on by promising that we would visit the cow on the way back.

There was a swishing in the crisp stalks and the terrier came hurtling through the orchard. Behind her were the two pups, both plunging nervously through the tall grass like tramp steamers in a heavy swell. Andrew gave a crow of delight and turned his attention to the dogs.

'Dadow 'n' baby putties,' he shouted. Dadow was his own improvisation upon the name Bambi, given to the terrier when she was a pup herself, no larger than a rat and fawn-like, with a timid, jittery-affectionate air.

I felt a certain contemptuous fondness for the dog. She had a faintly nauseating temperament, a refinement and daintiness which reminded me of one of those forty-ish withered spinsters who live genteel, shrinking lives in spas. In the social assessment of our times, her justification for existence was poor. Her attitude was that the world owed her a living, and she accepted with arrogant diffidence what was her due. I had seen her reclining on the hearth rug while a mouse scuttled about a couple of feet from her nose. She could not be honestly described as gainfully employed.

But Andrew was fond of her. He dragged her into his rough and tumble games, and she tolerated his boisterous love with a faded, suffering ennui. A fortnight after our arrival at Bereworde, when she was just over a year old, she gave birth to the two pups in one of the horse boxes. Who the father was, I could not decide. It must have been a big dog for the pups were already almost as tall as she. One, a bitch, had inherited her cravenly boot-licking temperament, its normal attitude being an ear-flattened, eye-rolling ingratiating stomach-wriggle. The other was very different. It was a dog and had the build of a bear cub. It was born with a thick woolly black coat that rapidly grew woolier and shaggier, until, at two months, it resembled an astrakhan muff.

Andrew's excitement at seeing the dogs was tempered with nervousness. He preferred the pups to be at a distance. Always they swamped upon him, skittling him over and standing on his chest licking his face while his screams scorched the air. I warded them off and we walked on across the meadow, the dogs following, past the smelly little pond with its crop of vile green surface and scribble of reeds. We met the wood-edge and followed it past the hunting gate down the broad slope.

I made no attempt to look at the base of the beeches in the escarpment areas and on the mossy logs for the famous snails. Nor was it the time of year for searching for the wood barley, a shade-seeking grass with a whiskery feather-like head on a tall erect stalk, which grew nowhere else in the county. I was far more attracted by the wood's bitten-about appearance, the sudden deep hollows over which young beeches precariously balanced, leaning like arm-flailing comic acrobats on a slack wire. The flint-scattered yellow and brown clay, and the soft chalk, was strewn with blackberry tendrils; in April these slopes, now ruddy with fern, would be dabbed with primroses, I guessed. Near the house the wood was sombre with firs, but here where the slope began to run down fast it was airy and gay with the lilt of rippling leaves and a pouring-in of the sky's light.

We did not go in for the ground was too steep and slippery for Andrew. We stood leaning against the fence, looking down into a great scoop edged by parallel rising cliffs and cut across by a sheer crumbly cliff; it was like a pit made by a gigantic shovel-stroke. Nearby was a dead beech, a branchless grey pylon of wood jutting like a shattered factory chimney from the compost of dark red leaves. It had been battered cruelly by woodpeckers. A million attacks upon its diseased bark were recorded in the close-meshed pattern of pockmarks. At the top, near the chewed, ragged tip, were seven holes. Two of them were the big round tunnels of green woodpeckers, but the others had been made by lesser spotted woodpeckers and were not more than two inches in diameter.

It was a good place to lean and smoke a cigarette, this, to let thoughts be dissolved with the earth's moisture by the sun's feeble heat, to follow in imagination the dazzling scurry of a grey squirrel across whipping branch bridges and down sheer boles, to watch the shift of shadows across settled leaves, and to listen to the morse code of tits. Andrew liked it there. He stood below me pressing with his hands on the wire and singing to himself, 'Baby, baby bunning, daddy don hunning,' which he sang to Amanda when her mother was washing and feeding her by the fire in the early evening.

The dogs were enjoying themselves too. When Bambi had plunged over the edge and raced down into the hollow, furrowing the leaves with her nose, the pups had stood together at the brink, whimpering with timidity, wanting to follow her but afraid of the height. Then the dog had cautiously slithered down, sliding most of the way on his rump, and the other had followed him. Now they were chasing madly about somewhere beyond the rim, where rabbit holes peppered the roadside bank, and their running paws made a continuous rustling sound in the breeze.

After a while we walked on. I whistled the dogs and they ran in line with us up and down the woodland wens. A hundred yards on the field ended, for here the wood turned abruptly in a sharp elbow, filling a narrow groove deeply with mixed firs, ash, holly and elder scrub. Out in the field was a tree that interested me. It was a Turkey oak, that had probably, decades ago, seeded from an acorn dropped by a wood pigeon. It was a bushy tree whose branches grew wide at the base, tapering to a pinnacle, with lined bark as grey and thick as elephant hide.

'Wait here a moment,' I asked Andrew and walked over to the oak. It was clearly over fifty years of age for scattered in the short grass were many of its bitter acorns in their stalkless scaly cups. From a distance it looked whole and robust, but on closer inspection I saw that it was diseased. Heart-rot had infected its core, eating through the sapwood and bast tubes, and destroying the inner layers so that new growth was retarded and the circulation of air and moisture ruined. Now there gaped in its side a long lobed hole and I knew that my guess had been right when, a week before, I had seen a little owl grasping something in its foot heading for the oak.

I picked up a dropped branch and tapped the trunk three times. Sure enough, the owl appeared, shooting out of the hole like a fawn cannonball from a muzzle. Death gave life; the tree decayed and in its wounds an owl would lay its eggs and rear its young. It was as I was watching the owl loping off towards the straggled line of wych elms in the centre of the pasture, that I heard Andrew yelling.

I strode quickly towards him and I heard above his crying the shrill screaming of one of the pups within the wood. Instantly I knew what had happened. I bent to Andrew, who was pointing helplessly to the wood and wailing over and over, 'Baby puttie cying, daddy, baby puttie cying.'

'Yes, I'm going to help it. Wait here like a good chap.'

He stood watching me tearfully as I ducked between the barbed strands of the fence and forced in the jungle of dead and half-strangled growth. The screaming led me straight to the pup. Bambi was dancing around her – it was the bitch – adding her yelps to the din, and the other pup was squatting in a patch of hellebore jerking its head in puzzlement from one side to the other.

As I had known, the pup was in a gin. It was held by the front leg, the steel teeth clamped just above its pad. I sweated and swore at the people who littered woods and hedges with the evil things, while I tried to force the jaws back with my hands. They were stiff with rust and the pup in her terror and agony bit me many times with her tiny sharp teeth. Finally I found a stout stub of wood, jammed it in and levered the trap open. The pup jerked herself out and hopped away, falling every time she tried to use the injured leg.

The gin might have been set months. It was worn and rusted, and the jaws met unevenly. It was half covered with the leaves of the previous autumn – they had probably been scattered over it by the trapper when he had set it – and its steel peg was deep in the black humus. I uprooted it and with a swing of the arm sent it spinning through the trees deep into a thorn brake where a magpie had been clattering a few minutes before.

Kneeling in the damp leaves I examined the pup's foot, while it squealed and threshed its tail. Fortunately it seemed to have been gripped in the end of the trap that barely met when the twisted hinge snapped together. The skin was torn and it was bleeding, but, as far as I could tell, no bones were broken. As I bound it up with my handkerchief I wondered how many hundreds of wild and domestic animals died prolonged deaths from cold and starvation in the gins that were tilled in Britain each month. In themselves they were inhuman instruments, but, worse, they were rarely used with even elementary consideration. Many trappers, I knew, did their rounds only once or twice a week, which meant that the rabbit or the stoat or the pheasant or the dog that was caught on the first or second day would have days and nights more of pain and misery before being mercifully clumped to death. I believed I knew who was responsible for this particular trap – a watery-eyed scrub-chinned fellow who lived in a cottage on the outskirts of Estodham, and who was often to be seen standing or moving furtively up Pedler's Hill, the hare pocket inside his shapeless jacket bulging with ferret, snares or gins.

Andrew was standing silent and white-faced when I scrambled through the fence again with Bambi and the other pup leaping excitedly around me. The bitch, which I carried in my arm, was trembling slightly but crouching unmoving against my chest.

I bent and showed him the bound paw. 'Baby puppy hurt her foot,' I told him. 'I had to wrap it up.'

Eyes wide with compassion, Andrew bent forward and stroked the flinching pied head. 'There, baby puttie, better now,' he said softly, and all the way across the meadow back to the house, which squatted comfortably, long and low, between the cedars, he kept telling me, 'Baby puttie hurt foot, daddy. Better now! Mmmm.'

The paw repaired in a few days and a week later the pup was scampering about on four legs. An evening or two after that I went out with a heaped tin plate to shut the dogs in the horse box for the night. When I whistled only Bambi and the hefty pup came running through the dusk. I whistled for a long time, walking down to the spinney and through the rookery trees that stood shining black in the moon's thin light, but there was no response.

The next day I went down to the Long Wood, across the lane into the land of Clementine Farm and across the common towards

Estodham, but the pup could not be found. It was never seen again. If it was lucky it might have been stolen by children and taken to a home with a hot range fire and liberal saucers of milk. On the other hand, it might again have ventured into a wood where the softness of the leaf run concealed a wide-set gin, there to stay until the jays found its stiff and dew-wet body.

Chapter Six

Our first family meeting was unexpectedly gloomy. When we had paid our preliminary visit Anna and Ian had told us frankly that Bereworde was faced with some big financial problems, but not until that evening did Bee or I realize precisely how big they were. I sat on the floor with my back against Bee's legs waiting for the families to arrive, studying the duplicated accounts for the past six months. It was a complicated document and my mind always hazes over at the sight of figures. After pressing laboriously through the first column I abandoned trying to reach detailed understanding. My eyes dropped to the last line and I read 'Excess expenditure over income: £334 4s.'. £334! My heart jolted. It seemed to me an enormous distance in the red. Of course they were all large figures – grocery bills for one month, for instance, amounted to over £100, and on the other side nearly £2,000 had been paid in rents during the six months. Even so, my eyes kept being dragged back with a dreadful fascination to that £334.

The meeting started and Aubrey formally presented the accounts. 'It's not been an easy matter getting these figures out,' he said, with a faintly accusing glance around the whole company. 'I don't vouch for their absolute accuracy. The difficulty has been taking into consideration the time lag of payment after the ordering or delivery of goods or performance of work that will have to be paid for. Also, as usual, it was impossible to find out the immediate position of rates and mortgage interest due. Anyhow, here they are for better or worse. And it's worse, I'm afraid.'

There was a glum silence while everyone stared at their sheets.

'Well, there doesn't seem any doubt that we simply *must* make *drastic* economies. Somewhere,' Anna said at last.

A dejected murmur of agreement.

Flora flourished a piece of paper. 'I've got something worked out here, Mr Chairman, if I can put it to the meeting. I've been rounding up the expenditure on coffee, cereals, soft drinks, greengroceries, cleaning materials and tea during the past month, and I calculate that they can all be cut, quite heavily. In fact we could save £17 4s. a month exactly on them.'

Hilary agreed. 'But I think we're going to have to have simpler meals all the way round. Sweet *or* soup. No coffee after dinner. Might even try no cooked breakfasts and no fruit for the vegetarians' breakfasts.'

This sounded extremely dreary to me. Already, I thought, Bereworde meals were not of a notably high standard.

'The point is,' Flora put in, 'the cost of living has gone up 10 per cent since the community started and the community's income has stopped still. Even dropped a bit, probably, though Aubrey would know that.'

'Yes, it has a bit,' he replied. 'Two families now here are paying a lower scale of rents than the families they replaced.'

There were a variety of other suggestions. Basil thought rents should be put up all round. Alec insisted that the community ought to trade with the Co-op to get 1s. 3d. dividend in the pound. There were also a number of improbable and impracticable money-raising ideas put forward, such as letting off the badminton hall to a village club. All that had to be done was to get a club started in the village.

'Wait, everyone! I think there is an alternative to both cutting spending and raising rents,' Aubrey said portentously.

'What's that – throwing Bereworde open as a stately home at a bob a nob?' John grunted.

Aubrey ignored him. 'A new spirit of efficiency is what is vitally necessary. So much money should be allocated to each department and each department should keep its own accounts, and they should be kept strictly up to date to show exactly what has been ordered as well as what has already been paid for. Food ought to be kept under tight control. People who go away and take rations with them ought to pay for them. Families ought not to be in arrears for more than one month, and everyone ought to be paying one month in advance. And people don't always pay for their guests, either. There ought to be a visitors' guest book kept.' He paused. 'If we went ahead on those sort of lines, with a little more organization and a little less chaos, I am perfectly certain we would soon be in daylight financially.'

'Well, I think what we need is a planning committee,' Gerald said flatly. 'I've said so all along and I shall go on saying so. Of course no-one's taken a scrap of notice. Not that I expect it. But now that it's obvious that we're in a mess – an unholy big mess – perhaps someone will listen to me. We want someone here with dictatorial powers. Someone who's going to be tough with people who won't act up to their responsibilities as members of the community. Why should people be able to skip their duties without being pulled up for it?' He cast a dark, eye-narrowed glance around, leaving one uncomfortably uncertain whether Gerald counted one a friend or an enemy. 'You all know my firm belief – that there should be a pair of co-ordinators, elected every three months, who during that time have got absolute power. That'd get things cracking and we'd soon be out of the mess.'

'Oh, Gerry, don't start that again,' Anna said wearily. 'It's entirely in opposition to all that Bereworde stands for and you can't see it.'

'Anarchy,' Gerald muttered blackly, 'that's what Bereworde stands for. Bloody anarchy.' He was a Berewordean by circumstance rather than choice. As Anna's brother he had been in from the start and his photography business was embedded inextricably in the community.

Talk continued in high spate for another hour and a half. Fuel troubles, moving the clothes line from the orchard to the pergola lawn, the possibility of getting a land-girl for the horticultural society, the cook crisis, buying a rotatiller, and a profusion of minor house matters were discussed and settled or not settled. They swirled around the looming central problem of the community's finances like satellites around a greater burning star. At first I had been following carefully, but after an hour or so I lost the trail amid the thickets of subsidiary and supplementary problems. Had any decisions to grapple with the threatened ruin been taken? I found myself wondering while talk buzzed around my head. I wasn't a bit sure that they had.

Ian had vanished twenty minutes ago. There was a kicking at the door and he came in bearing a vast tray stacked with mugs and plates. 'Tea up!' he called. 'Let's break it up here if we're going to start the conference.'

The conference was a yearly event. It was then that there was a retrospective review of the community's progress, and free discussion on the plans for its future. When everyone was grasping a mug of tea and chewing a cheese sandwich, Anna opened the discussion. I was not listening very closely at first. The talk about money had startled and alarmed me, but no-one else seemed especially worried. Ian, who carried the greater proportion of the financial responsibilities, was talking to Basil and roaring muffledly with laughter. Perhaps this was one of the blessings of the new life, an ability to achieve complete detachment from sordid money? I had not yet achieved that detachment. Remembrance of what had been said nagged disquietingly. Ah, well. I started on my sandwich and turned my attention to Anna.

'There's no need for me to go over all the early history, the real pioneering phase,' she was saying. 'Everyone here, even if he wasn't a party to it, knows it all. But there is one fundamental thing that has become clearer than ever to me during the past year. I'm now convinced that Ian and I made a major error right at the beginning. I'm sorry to say that we decided then not to put forward our own blueprint, our own design for living. We wanted to wait for each family to make its contribution and to see what would emerge. Candidly I think that what has emerged is a state of muddle, without any clearly defined motive for the existence of the community. I think that the time is long overdue for us to form a nucleus of agreement, to define our aims – and then go ahead and put them into practice. Of course there have been a lot of factors to take into consideration. Most of the families have come from different backgrounds and, perhaps, expected different things when they came here. We've all gone through a "growing pains" period, of accustoming ourselves to the social difficulties of living together. A thing that candidly I didn't foresee was the power of one individual to affect the mood of the whole community, and the way the personality of one person – or one family unit – brings a change of character to the whole community.' She smiled a trifle cautiously. 'I think everyone who was living here with the Crullters will know what I mean, and, of course, their leaving was inevitable. If they hadn't gone everyone else would have had to have gone. But now, despite this financial instability, I feel the community has reached a stage of reasonable temperamental balance and stability. Generally, I think the women get on better together than the men, and the children, after an initial stage of strangeness and insecurity, are benefitting enormously from this life. I think I'm right in saying that communal life has entailed more work than we all expected, and it has proved more expensive than we imagined it would be. But, all things considered, I'm certain we've resolved most of our early difficulties and that we can now start going ahead in a more adventurous and experimental way.'

There were murmurs that might have been approval or disapproval. 'Well, now, Ian, you're going to put forward your ideas for the future,' Jim said from the chair.

Ian, hunched in a corner with a cigarette pincered in his lips, shuffled through his pages of notes. 'Yes. First, I'm going to list what, in my view, we want and must achieve if Bereworde is to be a success in the long term. I'm framing this in a fairly general and material way. I think these are the things, a home, the easy chair, security and all that word involves, space for physical as well as spiritual development, and beauty. Now what have we already got? I would say we have companionship, the pleasure and the comfort of friends for ourselves and our children, an atmosphere of friendship, peace and tranquillity or excitement and adventure, as we need them, lightening the burden for the womenfolk —'

'Ha-ha,' Hilary laughed cynically and humourlessly.

'— and making for a general widening of interests. We also get stimulation of physical, cultural, mental activity and interests; and the fun of tastes shared among us all, grown-ups and children. I think we have those things in some measure, but only partly and imperfectly so far. What we have got to do, and what we have not yet experienced, is the fulfillment of continuous growth and development in ourselves.' He shuffled down more comfortably and put aside his notes. 'Now I believe the condition of success is that we must find in Bereworde something beyond our personal lives, we must enlarge social consciousness and our apprehension of the unit of which we are an integral part. Responsibility and unselfishness must be extended from the family to the whole unit. Natural consideration to others is the essence of real courtesy, but on the other hand I'm certain we must get to that happy stage where we feel able to say openly and honestly what we feel, and to criticize freely. We can only work and not give offence or cause unhappiness, we can only live harmoniously, if we are tolerant and understanding to the point of compassion. You must forgive me if I'm expressing all this in rather wide philosophical terms, but I am trying to put out ideas I find difficult to formulate. For me, our experiment here is set against the world and its history. I believe that history is a process of social growth and development not unlike that of any organism. There are periods when growth is slow and change almost imperceptible; there are others when you can see history being made under your eyes, and a world is revolutionized, in the historical time-scale, almost overnight. I believe we are passing through such a period now. The guiding philosophy for a group of men and women aware of those changes is to shape their lives by the shape of the things to come. "Tomorrow" should be a lovelier and more evocative word than "yesterday", and all our values should be measured by the yardstick of the future, not the past. It is that feeling for the future which should determine the emergence of a new leadership; and Bereworde should be one such experiment with time. I feel that we should agree on the fundamentals of some philosophy of living which would give our lives here the purpose and direction we all need.'

I was hesitant to put forward too forceful a view, as a raw freshman, but I felt compelled to say that as a new Berewordean, seeing the community with a certain objectivity, I could not yet perceive the broad basis of sympathy and agreement that both Anna and Ian wanted. Ian's philosophy was attractive but how was it to be, how could it be, applied in a practical way? I stopped there. I did not express the continuation of my thoughts, which was that, although I liked most of the Bere-wordeans and so far was enjoying the communal life, the community seemed to me to be fragmented. We ate together and we co-operated on a good many household and estate tasks, but I had not yet consciously felt the harmony and unity of ideals and objectives that had been so heavily stressed — except on that one day when we worked together to bring in the cherry. Each family appeared to me to have its own private reason for living there, but those reasons did not cohese into a way of living together; they were essentially private and half concealed.

Gerald immediately brought the discussion down to ground with a bang. As always, he projected his dominant idea of the moment like a battering ram. What Bereworde needed, he insisted, was a centralized organization with one person in charge, then sat back sucking a cold pipe threateningly.

Ham Sullivan, who a week before had announced in the dining-room that he was thinking of leaving Bereworde because he could not stand the bickering and back-biting, said that in future the selection of families with strong individualistic or difficult personalities should be considered most carefully.

There were some enthusiastic expressions of support to that, but Ham did not appear to take them personally.

'Well, it's a pioneer effort,' Gladys Morris said, 'and there are bound to be failures. I think what would help would be a more general use of the library. You can sit there a whole evening without seeing a soul.'

'And look what happened to my plans for play-reading and a debating society last winter,' Aubrey put in plaintively. 'Everyone egged me on and then no-one ever turned up.'

Eventually the meeting passed on to the formation of a one-year plan. I looked at the agenda. Items listed under this heading were: (1) Provide accommodation for one family by converting the loft over the stables; (2) Redecorate children's dining room and convert lobby into bathroom for Jim and Mary; (3) Paint outside of house (agreed to obtain 15 gallons of paint); (4) Paint and repair water tower; (5) Amenities, i.e., hard court, rationalization of gardens; (7) Horticultural Society, hedges and cold frames; (8) Hot water system and water softener; (9) Food production. It did not take as long as I expected. It was agreed that Ian, Alec and Jim, with Julian as a weekend member, should form a sub-committee to draw up proposals for the one-year plan in detail. Next came the winter programme. Aubrey suggested a fresh effort to form groups, physical, covering games, table tennis, squash, etc.; cultural, covering music, play reading etc.; and political, covering guest speakers and debates.

'I would like to have a regular meeting open to the village once a month,' Anna said. 'I think it would help to create a good relationship with the village. It's not all it should be, as everyone knows.'

Chapter Seven

The monthly meeting open to the village never came to pass. Until the end the relationship with the village remained as patchy, imperfect and surreptitiously antagonistic as it had been from the beginning.

Estodham was an unbalanced community. The old village was a small group of cottages around a triangular green, on to which the Plumes Inn and the three shops faced. But five hundred yards to the north there began a thick belt of suburban houses which stretched along the Downsteeple road for over a mile. It was here that most of the enmity to Bereworde was located. Relations with the true villagers were friendly. A number of them worked casually for the community. Ted Vickers helped in the evenings and at weekends in the horticultural society. Mrs Tompkins came up to do the sewing. Odd-jobbing, mostly carpentry – repairing furniture destroyed by the children – was done by Mr Hooper, a slaughterman at the downland zoo. One or another of the village girls was usually helping in the kitchen.

But the suspicion of the middle-class element flared into active hatred when it became known that the people who had moved into the manor were a bunch of bolsheviks. During the four years of the community's existence, a constant stream of scandal filtered back to our ears. Free-love was practised and there was a rota system for the exchange of wives among the men. The children were filthy and diseased, and spent all their time playing erotic games. Drunken parties went on until the early hours every weekend. And, of course, the house was a key-point in the Soviet Union's plan for world revolution. An inspired series of variations were composed around these classical themes. It was an attitude that was basically political, a resentment, a bitter conviction that the Berewordians were traitors to their class; but it also had roots in the Englishman's distrust of and hostility towards anything that deviates a degree from the conventional.

On one occasion there was a Conservative meeting at the village hall which was addressed by a doctor who had advanced from new radio fame, achieved by means of a chummy growl, into the political field. He was the prospective Tory candidate for a neighbouring constituency. Several Berewordeans went down to the meeting and after it was over walked across the road to the Plumes for a drink.

In the bar was a group of local Conservatives gathered around the eminent doctor, and as Harry and Chris Barlow and Ham and Margit Sullivan entered, one of the detached villa housewives was telling him about the *lumpenproletarian* squalor that had infected the gracious atmosphere of the manor. 'It really is shocking,' she was saying, 'the way those wretched children are treated. And they're all in a terrible state physically. They get nothing to eat except raw cabbage and they look half-starved.'

Harry, whose temperament was fiery and impulsive, pushed through the crowd. 'It might be of interest to you to know that I live at Bereworde and that I've been a nurse for twelve years, and you couldn't find a healthier crowd of children anywhere.'

Casting around frantically for the right words, Margit followed with a spray of broken English. 'I haf just come from America and there there are no better children. They are warnderfully healthy at Bereworde.' (This was some time before she and Ham fell finally out of love with the community.)

There was some muted argument from the Conservative group and eventually Alec, who had joined the Berewordeans, said: 'It might interest you to see the place for yourself. Come up for a drink.'

He smiled benignly. 'I probably wouldn't get out alive. Besides I've heard those sort of invitations thrown out before.'

'All right, I'll write formally and invite you,' Alec said.

The next day a polite letter of invitation was sent to the doctor, and a couple of afternoons later he drove up. He was shown around by Anna and afterwards there was a gathering for cocktails in the Parfitts' room. Everyone was eager to answer his questions and he was sweetly charming and courteous. Eventually he said, 'Well, your children are healthy enough and it's a very nice place. I think you're a lot of cranks, of course, but I suppose the stunt has its points.'

The doctor's reasons for accepting the invitation were probably a natural personal curiosity. At that time Ian was active in the local Labour Party. Not long after he was adopted as prospective candidate. His opponent was not the doctor, who was fighting the next constituency, but throughout the 1950 general election campaign there were Conservative platform references to people who would undermine the basis of family life, who attacked the sacredness of the home with profane and alien ideas, and so on.

Whatever the doctor reported back to his village supporters, it made no difference to the sustained vilification of all that Bereworde represented. Typical of the attitude was that displayed when Bee made her monthly visit to the clinic with baby Amanda. She went with Gladys Morris, whose new baby had not been gaining. After Gladys's baby had been weighed, Bee heard a comment whispered by one waiting mother to another, 'Of course, it's a Bereworde baby, the poor little thing. What can you expect?' Five minutes later the same mother was cooing admiringly over Amanda's lusty pneumatic body. The fact that Amanda, too, was a Bereworde baby was irrelevant. One was underweight and that was because it had been reared at Bereworde; the other was a fine baby, which was an isolated, disconnected fact.

Anna's attitude was that the anti-Bereworde faction should not be allowed to get away with it. They dominated the Women's Institute, so a counterbalancing influence was introduced. She, Flora, Hilary and Bee became members, and attended fairly regularly. Superficially there was a friendly atmosphere, and a genuine friendliness was shown by a few of the members. However, that did not prevent a member of the committee telling a story of Anna's interview with a prospective under-gardener, to whom, it appeared, she had talked wearing 'nothing but a whisp of chiffon'. It was funny, but irritating, too. Each year the Berewordeans put on an entertainment for the Institute's Christmas show at the village hall. I wrote the script for the next show and in it, Anna, who was being given an audition by impresario Alec Cameron, on being complimented upon her tap-dance turn, replied dramatically, 'Ah, but you should see me doing it dressed in nothing but a whisp of chiffon.' The face of the inventive committee member, who was sitting in the front row, remained stoically expressionless, but the gust of laughter that went through the hall was evidence that the point had been felt.

As was the case with most other Berewordeans, I was on amicable terms with Estodham, both sides, on an individual level; but to the end there was no mellowing, no compromise by the suburban set in their basic detestation of the Bereworde community.

There was another more esoteric aspect of village life. The vicar was a remarkable and interesting man. Originally a Methodist minister, he had been ordained in the Church of England in 1927, and later had begun, casually, to read psychology. The casual interest strengthened into a serious study. A few years later he founded a psychiatric clinic in London, and then one in Downsteeple. I never satisfactorily settled how he reconciled his Freudian beliefs with his religion, and found him elusive and metaphysical on this matter. He visited Bereworde several times, a small, shrunken, wrinkled man who reminded me of that elfin film Irishman, Barry Fitzgerald, but he had an aura of kindly wisdom that made understandable the respect and love that was felt for him in the village. To an extent, he suffered similar suspicion and sneering as did Bereworde from the stockbrokers and their wives, but that did not appear to impinge upon his calm self-containment. Around him there had grown up a small colony of people who had originally come to him for treatment. One of them was Gerald's closest friend, Bill Carr-Forbes. He was the son of a wealthy London art-dealer and had been invalided out of the Army. It was he who went around in the battered grey Frazer Nash. With his check hacking jacket, narrow-bottomed flannels, suede boots, yellow waistcoats and flattened cap, he achieved an Osbert Lancaster cartoon exactness of the race-track road-house type of rich young idiot, whose natural environment is martinis and women of flat and exhausted beauty. Yet the life he lived gave the lie to that external picture. He worked as a farm labourer, was sidesman at the church, gravedigger and bellringer. He lived in a caravan parked in the meadow beside the Plumes. True, the caravan did bear a likeness to the Mayfair apartment that seemed his proper background: green fitted carpet, cocktail cabinet, electric record-player and refrigerator.

Another of the vicar's patients was a young ex-Etonian with a gaudy history of rebellion and petty crime, who worked as a factory hand. Later he left to study painting in Paris. There was also a curate who stayed to receive treatment from the vicar, and who spent most of his time up at Bereworde. He was a pleasant young man, tortured by shyness, who told me one day that he had a brother-fixation, which seemed to me to be a novel variation.

Never before or since have I encountered such a concentration of neurotics. Apart from one or two people at Bereworde itself who were being or who had recently been psychoanalysed, one found that an extraordinary number of the villagers were being sorted out emotionally by the vicar. Yet I know that he did bring happiness and confidence to several badly lopsided people, people who until he came to Estodham had heard only vaguely of psychoanalysis and regarded it as a sort of crackpot, crooked witch-doctory. It is a pity that more clergymen do not extend their work into this arena of practical and pellucid Christianity.

Chapter Eight

A child does not adjust itself to new surroundings with the surface ease of an adult. Andrew had spent nearly two years of expanding and quickening consciousness in an atmosphere that, despite our efforts to insulate it, had been charged with tension and suppression. The change to a home where children's happiness was allowed to flower freely was too much for him to grapple with. The children were noisy and they ran and yelled; there were no restrictions on leaving the room, or where and at what he could play. Already nervously uncertain of how he stood with people, his reaction to Bereworde was sharply to draw in within himself. He stood on the edge of life and plainly was not going to step into the ring until he was absolutely certain that the move would not be followed by instant rebuff.

He was happy enough in the family circle, happier than we had seen him before. If Bee was within reach he would try almost anything that was being done by the other children. Out with me in the meadow below the boundary fence, he skipped along with the wind blowing his thick curly dark hair. But he refused to experiment alone. He knew where he was safe. We had no intention of forcing him. He would have to convince himself that he could safely cast away the armour shell of caution. In the meantime we were ready to put up with an increased clingingness and reluctance to be separated from us, even at meal-times. It was as if he were beginning to doubt the sense of his own attitude and was deliberately intensifying it to reassure himself it was right.

On a quite normal level his fears were reasonable. Bereworde was a big place and the separation between Bee in one room and Andrew in the garden was a wide one. And, in the way that every nervous child who shows his nervousness must pay, Andrew paid. One or two of the older children quickly saw that he could be pushed around, and they literally did that. Helplessly he would stand sobbing without making a gesture against Timmy Parfitt or Brian Cameron who had just grabbed a toy from his hand. He made efforts to form a relationship with the other children on his own timorous terms. While they racketted with their tricycles up and down the corridor he would stand fearfully in the doorway of our room, trying to tempt one or other of them in by offering them sweets or dates. Usually the bribes were snatched and the invitation ignored, and Andrew would sadly shut the door and return to his solitary games. It was a painful period for him, and painful for us also.

But there was one matter which we felt called for positive and immediate action. Between Bee entering hospital to have Amanda and the move to the community, Andrew had developed a peculiar revulsion against dirt. He played, fastidiously, but the moment that his hands became soiled a wail would start and he would be rushing in crying, 'Hands dirty, mummy, hands dirty,' and was content only when they had been washed. At bedtime the suit he had been wearing all day was taken off with barely a smudge on it.

In one sense that was most satisfactory. It was useful and labour-saving to have such a shiningly clean child, and in the eyes of relatives and visitors it was highly commendable. 'Haven't you got an angelic child! I wish mine kept as clean as yours.' Perhaps, but contrarily Bee became increasingly worried about it.

She interrupted my work one evening and brought in cups of coffee for us both. 'I wish I could make up my mind what to do about this,' she said. 'There's something definitely wrong. All the children were having a wonderful time this afternoon in the sandpit. It had been raining and it was gloriously sloshy and they were plastered with wet sand. But Andrew wouldn't go near. He obviously *wanted* to play with them. He ran upstairs to get his spade and bucket, but when he came down he just stood on the edge dithering miserably. I could see him fighting it out with himself, and in the end the clean Andrew won. If *only* I could see why. He never used to be like this. I wonder if it was anything that happened while he was in the residential nursery and I was having Amanda?'

'It may have been, but when I went to collect him he seemed happy enough and the matron said that apart from dirtying his bed a couple of times, he'd been as good as gold.'

Bee stopped with a match half way to a cigarette. 'Of course,' she said slowly. 'What an idiot I am not to have seen that before. I can just see it happening. Andrew dirties his bed and he's told he's a dirty little boy – probably no more than that; no slaps even – and, as he always does, he takes it deeply to heart. Result: ever after dirt of any kind is something to be ashamed of, something that brings disapproval.'

'Why, yes, I think you may be right. It sounds logical, the way he would react to an experience like that. But what's the cure?'

She was silent for a few moments. 'I don't know yet but I'm going to try something tomorrow.'

Next morning Bee took a large bowl out on to the terrace. She filled it with earth and then poured in water from a jug until it was soup of mud. All this time Andrew had been watching her, fascinated. 'What's that for, mummy?' he kept asking.

'It's for you, darling. Now look, here's your bucket. You have some fun with this lovely mud.'

For several minutes he stood looking dubiously from her to the bowl, and then hesitantly bent and began patting at the mess with his spade. The moment that it splashed on to his blouse he leaped back with a whimper. For ten minutes Bee crouched there encouraging him, telling him it was lovely mud, that it was great fun to get thoroughly dirty, that she'd loved getting dirty when she was a little girl, and not to bother about his clean suit. Dubiously, reluctantly, even, he began filling his pail, every now and then darting incredulous glances at Bee. Then, suddenly, as if something was cut free, the uncertainty vanished and he began absorbedly scooping it up with the pail and heaping it in a running slimy heap between his legs, and for the first time he seemed not to be noticing that it was smearing his sandals and legs.

An hour later when Bee went back he was black. And happy. He greeted her with a shout and laughed, 'Aren't I having a lovely time, mummy? Look, I've made a great big castle here.' Then he lunged back into the bowl, with the mud reaching up to his elbows.

It was the end of Andrew's inhibition about dirt. He did not develop a morbid passion for dirt; he merely became healthily uncaring about cleanliness. No longer was the horror of getting dirty a barrier to joining in games with the other children.

It also helped to free him in other directions. Gradually he began to submit less and less willingly to terrorism, and the rebellion dated from the mud bowl initiation. It was satisfying to me when not long after I walked down the kitchen passage to find him having a stand-up row with Timmy. They were both near tears and yelling at the tops of their voices as they grappled with a scooter, but Andrew got it and he delivered a hacking punch at Timmy's ribs as he reeled against the wall. It was probably unethical of me to interfere but I could not restrain myself from patting him on the bottom and whispering 'Good chap' as I passed.

To understand the problems of children one has to stoop and see them from their height, not use superior adult knowledge. It is the foggy complexity of the adult mind, with too much experience and too little understanding of that experience, that is the cause of miseducation. Simplicity and clarity are the things which society seems to set out methodically to destroy in the child, and almost always succeeds. It was some time later that Andrew showed signs of what I at first thought to be cruelty.

Every year the villagers trooped up to Bereworde with their rusty twelve and fourteen bores to indulge in the happy slaughter of young rooks. I did not care much for the idea. I was always prepared to shoot for my dinner – and to shoot ruthlessly the grey squirrels that stole eggs and munched the sprigs of young trees; but I rebelled at mass killing for sport. Nor, in the case of the rooks, was I convinced of the necessity for thinning numbers. Intensive research has not shown conclusively that the rook is the farmer's enemy. It eats a great deal of grain but it also eats a great many wireworms. Which one outweighs the other has not been settled.

Afraid that Andrew might be upset by the massacre of his rooks I tried to explain that men were coming to shoot some because they were thought to steal a lot of wheat. He had seemed a little dismayed, but during the shoot he was out there yelling with excitement as one bird after another flopped through the branches to earth. Afterwards he came running, red-faced with pleasure, brandishing a dead young rook, shouting: 'Look, daddy, it's deaded! BANG.' For a long time after that he was throwing it up in the air, jabbing a stick skyward and growling 'bang-bang' as it tumbled down.

It was next day that he came up to where Bee and I were sitting on the lawn. He was running carefully with his hand stretched out. 'Look, daddy, mummy, a ladybird,' he cried excitedly. He stood beside us, watching the glossily varnished insect toiling up his wrist. 'Isn't it a nice little ladybird?' he breathed.

Then he shook it off, and stamped on it.

'Is it dead now, daddy?' he asked.

I was silent for a second. I shot a quick look at Bee and then said casually? 'Yes, old boy, it's quite dead now.'

When he had gone I said to her: 'What do you do about that?' I knew that in itself it was a trivial incident, but I saw it against the background of Andrew's flowing love for all living things. His cold-blooded destruction of the ladybird was a shock: and there was his full-blooded enjoyment of the rook-shoot yesterday. . . . Yet I did not want to make the mistake of planting false ethical standards in his mind. Men *did* shoot birds and usually believed themselves to have a sound, moral reason for doing so. It would be absurd to present it to Andrew as a brand of adult naughtiness. I wanted him to perceive life's realities truthfully, not to have them distorted by adult prejudices into artificial shapes of good and evil. It was all quite simple, seen from his uncomplicated viewpoint. A gun made a loud noise. It had the power to knock over a distant object. Both magical and intoxicating things to a small boy. I was confident that his attitude towards killing would quite naturally rationalize itself. It was the child who had been badly frustrated who pulled wings off flies, I told myself, in revenge against his parents not the fly. Even so, the ladybird incident seemed to be in a different category. 'Was he being cruel, I mean was he enjoying killing it?' I asked Bee.

'No, I don't think so,' she said. 'Did you see his face? There was no enjoyment in it but he was looking very absorbed. He's beginning to get curious about death in the same way he is about birth. Killing the ladybird was an experiment, a handy way of giving himself an illustration of the difference between being alive and being dead.'

I felt that Bee was right. Cruelty is not an instinctive thing. No child is cruel unless it has been made to strangle some strong emotion that should have had natural outlet. Next day I was sure she was right. I came upon Andrew standing beside Amanda's pram beside the shrubbery. He was showing her something on his finger and I heard him saying: 'Pretty caterpillar, isn't it, Manda?' as he watched it humping along his bare arm. 'Mustn't hurt it,' as she grabbed for it. 'We'll put it back now.'

With great tenderness he lifted it on to a leaf of bramble.

Chapter Nine

Christmas began for me on the afternoon of Christmas Eve day, crawling like a Metro-Goldwyn-Meyer Cherokee through frost-sharp raspberry canes, chopper in one hand and cudgel in the other, in pursuit of three ducks and six chickens. It had been somebody's misconceived idea to isolate the table birds in the fruit cage. On that day John and I went down to slay them.

An ancestral wildness had revived within the birds during their imprisoned freedom in the shrubby enclosure. The ducks displayed unsuspected resource, but their evasive rushes were clumsy, their wits sluggish, compared with the chickens' wiles. Mudded, exhausted, scratched, out of temper, we quartered the fruit cage uncountable times, sometimes creeping stealthily, at other times lumbering furiously through the spiky tangles. Subdued fretful clucking came from the depths of undergrowth, and every now and then a bulky brown body would hurtle like a shell in a frenzy of noise between our legs or under our arms. The last survivor was at last captured, as dusk was sinking into night, burrowed beneath a thick bush. Wearily we trudged back to the house, our arms aching from the weight of the corpses.

Lights were streaming from the house into the bleak winter wind. There seemed to be a great deal of disorganized activity around the kitchen. Bee and Anna were adding to a hillock of mince pies on the dresser, Flora was icing a cake, Harry and Sylvia, the kitchen maid, were clearing up the afterbirth of an earlier cooking operation. As I entered the light and warmth I relaxed, glad to be back in the quickening festival stream. Flora looked up and, with icing funnel dropping a pink worm on the floor, said: 'You've come just in time. The pump's packed in. There's no water.'

John swore heavily. We piled the birds on a chair and tramped out again, across the stable yard and into the engine room. The wide leather belt was wavering steadily around the steel drum; the electric motor was thrumming placidly. Everything looked all right – but no water was coming up. I switched off and stood leaning against a bench to take the weight off my bad leg, wriggling my toes in the wetness of my sock, while John banged and jerked at the motor. He swore again and, ducking, vanished through the wire-fenced archway into the dimness of the bore-hole chamber. More knocking and a prolonged scraping sound. I switched on at his command. There was a momentary throb of machinery, the belt heaved, the wheel spun into action. John reappeared. 'Well, we can write that off,' he said, thrusting a greasy hand through his hair. 'Not a drop coming up. Come on, we'd better get the emergency pump going. God knows how long it's been like that. I expect they emptied the bloody tank before thinking of looking in here.'

The emergency pump, a smaller, simpler apparatus, was housed deep in the cellar of the house where the air was poisonous with coke fumes from the boiler. It seemed quite logical and inevitable that that would not work either. For an hour and a half John wrestled with it, while I held a torch, passed over screwdrivers, spanners and oilcan. Periodically I threw over the switch to an alarming firework shower of blue sparks while John violently swung the flywheel. We tried weighting the arm-platform with roped together cans of paint. The extra weight appeared at first to help but it did no permanent good.

Glaring at me through a shag of hair, his chin daubed with black, John growled: 'This is getting monotonous. I know what someone's going to suggest, but I'm not bloody well doing it.' I had heard that the previous Christmas also the pumps had failed and John had started off at midnight in a misfiring old Cadillac to drive four hundred miles, to Hull and back, to get a vital spare part.

Aubrey had arrived home when we walked back into the kitchen. He stared at us with round ominous eyes when we broke the news to everyone. 'This is the end of Bereworde,' he exclaimed dramatically. 'We shall have to evacuate for Christmas.' He imaginatively enlarged on the crisis during dinner: obviously the spring had been exhausted, the flow across those deep sandwiches of chalk had drained. Nature would drive us out where a harsh economic system had failed. We must all make our plans for the retreat. . . . His anxiety was shared by us all, but a way out was seen.

While washing up was being done in a puddle of amber water, coaxed in a slow dribble from the bottom of the tank, Gerald rang up the police station. We were all plucking birds in the kitchen when he came in and said: 'It's all right. The Fire Brigade's coming with a water tender.'

There was a loud cheer and someone tossed in the air a carnival snow-storm of feathers.

'Well, we'd better start getting ready for another dozen guests for Christmas,' said Harry, not suspecting how prophetic she was being.

'We shall be safe if Father Christmas's beard catches alight, anyway,' Gladys remarked.

Aubrey went to unpack his emergency suitcase.

The news of the pending rescue relaxed the atmosphere considerably and a new animation ran through the house. Yet I was left still feeling a little apprehensive and worried. We were safe for Christmas, but Aubrey might well be right. Suppose that due to some dark subterranean trauma the spring had died? That, surely, would be the death-blow to the community. Boreholes could not be sunk for ninepence. Even if we had ninepence to spare. I tugged faster at the duck's feathers and drove away the thoughts. Once again I seemed apart from most of the Berewordeans in my concern about such practical problems.

As usually seemed to happen at Bereworde arrangements lagged grossly behind schedule, but that did not matter much on Christmas Eve. At about eleven-thirty all energy was canalized on to the hall. A labour corps had been busy bringing in the yule logs, great cylinders of pine and red chunks of the cherry tree. The huge iron fire basket was banked high and the inglenook was like the maw of a furnace. Julian, his friend Tony, another film director, Alec and Ian had brought in the Christmas tree. It was a 20-foot-high spruce, cut in the spinney, that had been roped in position in the window bay, and now it was being festooned with decorations. Long voluminous yellow curtains had been hung across the staircase. The radiogram was playing Woody Herman's idea of *Jingle Bells*. Anna, Bee and one or two others were sitting in a lake of coloured paper and boxes preparing the children's tree presents. Holly and mistletoe, poached by me and John from the woods of Hoo Hall, were being arranged around the wall light brackets, and Flora, balanced precariously on a chair, was arraying the candelabra with glittering silver paper.

There was a screech of brakes and a swing of headlights outside on the forecourt, and the reassuring news telegraphed round that the fire engine had arrived. Half a dozen men had come on a water tender and they finished stocking up the roof tank just as the rum punch was wheeled in. At one-thirty everyone was in the hall, including the firemen, eating hot mince pies and drinking punch around the fire. I was feeling a little light-headed with tiredness and alcohol. Bee's eyes looked heavy and she had synthetic snow on her hair. I squeezed her hand. She smiled and said: 'Isn't this nice?' I was thinking the same. I felt warm-hearted towards everyone present and delightfully sentimental. The radiogram was softly playing carols: *On the first day of Christmas my true love said to me*. I looked round at the hall, a shimmer of brilliant crackerbox colours, a glow of dark panelling, the shuddering light of the fire swarming up the dusky winterwood green of the spruce, illuminating for a fantastic second the tinsel fairy on the top. Everyone looked untidy and tired and cosy, and talk was now subdued and muted after the exciting hours. I talked for a few minutes to a fireman who told me about another Christmas during the war, of a children's party in a London tube station, jellies and sweets for those who feared bombs even on that day, and for those whose homes were rubble, gone for all Christmases. I thought of Andrew asleep upstairs and of the delight of tomorrow for him – for me, too, because, as before, I had begun by reluctantly accepting the inevitability of Christmas and had ended by surrendering utterly to its enchantment.

It was work mostly next day, work and a thrum of activity. Parties and meals and firewood and washing-up and winding up clockwork toys and bringing in the long teak table-top from the stables and collecting brass candlesticks from the families for the evening dinner. A lull of secret closeted preparation, and then at eight-thirty everyone – hardly recognizable in long frock or disinterred dinner suit – was gathering for cocktails, and dinner was ready: thirty of us down the long table, wine and candlelight and oversized helpings of duck and chicken.

The firemen arrived punctually for the party. It was another squad this time, but they had evidently been briefed by their mates as to what to expect. They were in their party-best uniforms and their hair gleamed with Brylcreem, and as soon as they had finished the tiresome business of replenishing the tank, they were dancing zestfully to Bill Carr-Forbes's jazz records. Three or four village couples had crossed no man's land and joined the community festivities and Bill had brought over a car-load of 20-year-olds from Burksted. The hall was packed and guests overflowed into the library, and there were one or two excursions into private rooms and out to the lodge for off-shoot parties. Friends of mine who had come down I saw occasionally over the rim of a glass across the room or as a familiar face swirling past me on the dance floor. For the first time since being carried into hospital six years before I was daring to try a stiff-legged quickstep, and I was enjoying it even if my stump was sore and aching.

At past two o'clock I pushed through the curtains and opened the front door. The firemen had gone with their tender and the gravel was deserted, palely golden in the light of the fanged stars. Long carpets of light were cast across it from the tall windows. I walked beyond them until I could no longer hear the music and the wave-sounds of voices, on to the dark crisp grass beneath the beeches. It was an iced, windless, rigid silence of a winter night. I walked slowly, feeling the twigs dropped by the nesting rooks of the previous March crunching beneath my shoes. The air numbed my flesh. A tremulous hollow note came from the Long Wood, the signal of a tawny owl, and its cry seemed to be one that had sounded throughout my life, from boyhood when I had walked across the wide moonlit sea of grass of Osterley Park to stand, satisfied with my loneliness in the cold darkness, beside the lakes and listen for owls, and also in the hope of again seeing there a hunting otter. The hooting trailed away, and then the quiet was split by a searing *keer-wick keer-wick*, answered distantly by another such call, as the owl flew invisibly overhead. I turned and looked back at the house, starred by its own lights, a core of radiance and warmth in the bareness of the Chiltern hills, and I was happy to remember that I had become part of the continuity of life that its walls had contained for so long. This was a mythical Christmas, of a sort that seemed detached from the year it was ending and the age that had no place for the country house and its ancient compact, interwoven social pattern.

I was glad that I had seen one Christmas like this, for not even the gaiety of the past hours that still clung around me like October gossamer and which was to be returned to could disperse the foreboding that Europe would not see many more. My hand, seeking a cigarette packet in my pocket, met a wired woolliness, and I laughed aloud as I recalled sneaking out of the kitchen door a few hours before and arriving at the front, bearded and red-dressing-gowned, to be greeted by the whoops and shrieks of the children, and then the hush of stupified wonderment as I unhooked presents from the spruce's branches. Suddenly I wanted to be back in the party; it seemed set firmly for day; and I walked rapidly back feeling on my face the soft dab of the first snow of Christmas.

Chapter Ten

I had spent the whole of the previous evening repairing the car hood with rubber cement and strips of webbing. The fabric, rotten with successive soakings and dryings, so that the elasticity had gone from the weave, had finally split with a noise like a jay's screech a few days before. We had been driving back from a rare trip to the cinema in Downsteeple, across the downs where orange and blue gliders soared like buzzards on summer days and where recently a pair of Montagu's harriers had nested (but their eggs were taken by schoolboys). Always powerful winds blew here, winds which came charging across the wide valley from the outpost hills of the long range. The lean little thorns that wriggled across the top-level fields or stood in conspiring clumps on the southern slopes showed that. They were sculptured by the winds, frozen into dragged-out postures, like current-combed reeds seen through clear waters of a river. The acid gusts killed buds and tender shoots on the windward side, and pressed the growing branches down and forward. The bushes were dwarfed and it was hard to find one more than three feet high on the open sweeps. They were liked by birds. Magpies nested in them, almost filling them with their solid stick snowballs, and the wheatears which nested in the rabbit burrows dug in the thin-turfed chalk, used them in their chain of flitter-hopping posts, bowing and *tut-tutting* from the head branches.

The wind was blowing hard and cold across the night sky. After climbing in wavy gradients for three miles the road flattened and swung along the brink of a steep drop down to the valley. As soon as we topped the crest, where stars were cascading on a dark satinny chute, I knew that something was going to happen. The hood had been slapping against the struts with a rippling, crackling noise, and when we met the full force of the wind it ballooned ominously. Quickly I twisted the hand throttle and cut down to forty, but it was too late. Several separate tearing sounds ran into one long rasp and the hood's halves sagged inside the car, the front half draping across my head and around the bucket seat, and strips snicked about in the wind-like thongs. It took four tubes of rubber cement and a lot of webbing to piece it together again. I had reached the point where I was doubting the sense of spending more money on the car. Under my ownership it had had a life almost as adventurous, within a narrower orbit, as during its Army years. It had been dug out of a north Devon beach before an advancing tide; it had crawled between boulders on a Skiddaw pass; it had struggled along Land's End in an April storm that threatened to swipe it up and give it to the sea; it had come through floods and snow with little more than a wet carburettor. But the three years had left their mark. Now the engine ran with an angry clatter and rust had got a hold on the wing flanges. The day of ultimate dissolution could not be long delayed. I patched the hood myself, working in the barn alongside Gerald's 'Leaf', the triple-carburettor Lea Francis that crouched like a grey cat.

After the previous night's laborious business of smearing on the cement, which stuck in hard black clots to the skin, and delicately positioning the ragged jig-saw of the hood, I was hesitant to risk undoing the work. Yet it was such a seductively blithe day that I could not resist dropping the hood. I backed out the car into the stable yard, loosened the two windscreen nuts and gently concertinaed the hood. There was a soft crunching sound but it seemed still to be in one piece. I swung the windscreen over so that it lay flat along the bonnet and drove slowly past the spinney and out into the lane.

It was an unbelievable day. The date was 27 January; the weather belonged to the April extolled by English poets in other lands. Driving down the steep curling narrowness of Pedlar's Hill was like skimming down a ski-run. The sunlight rippled in sparkling wavelets down the land; the bare blackthorns seemed wine-dipped; the green hazel catkins were little lanterns, each holding a small pale flame. The land swept down with me, great benevolent curves of pink-shining fallow and pasture of freshest green, with manes of dark woodland tossing back in the wind's rush.

I twisted the throttle and threw the car on. It was exhilarating to feel the torrent of keen air, to plunge down into the brilliance like a diver into deep silver water. There was added piquancy in the memory of the BBC's seven o'clock weather forecast – of fog in the London area. I thought of the raw blurr-edged cavern of Fleet Street and exulted again in the freedom of the sun and the opening year.

Quickly the views flattened. The Beacon was out of sight now and the encircling tract of valley bottom, with its crystally distinct farm buildings, elm trees and hedge-stitched fields, was hidden by the looming height of the opposite ridge. I crossed the main road and set the car up the long stiff climb through National Trust land to Little Gadeley. The lane began to elbow out to the south, to bend round the great park of Ashcroft, formed in Norman times so that boars and deer might be hunted freely. The thousand acres of beech and oak scattered land was crossed by wide grassy rides that had been mediaeval public roads. It was country of ancient pattern, a pattern that had been evolved by tyranny, infliction, often ruthless cruelty. The quicks, that gave form and composition to fields and haven to blackbirds, bullfinches and whitethroats, were a consequence of the Enclosures, of the dispossession of the peasantry and the yeoman freeholders from their open-field shots and selions. The great park of Ashcroft had been formed from wilderness of heath and scrubland, but it had also enclosed large areas of demesne land put down to grass, which had meant unemployment for the landless labourers. The sun seemed to illuminate for me the ancient human conflict and suffering that had fashioned the beauty that was now here and of which I was so consciously glad to be a part.

Nor had change stopped. I pulled up on the brow of the hill and stared with rising anger at the 'bottom' or dell at the side of the lane. Into it had surged a wood of mature beeches. They came down the facing slopes like an army of tall strong men; last autumn their massed foliage had been a cascade of fire; in another two months the yellow-freckled purple flowers would have hung like tassels on a heavy green curtain. That was how it would have been. Now the slope was bare but for a few spindly saplings not worth felling and the stumps, gleaming white discs, among the litter of brash on the minced-up ground. Sprawling obliquely up the rise where it had rolled with the cross-saw that had severed its hold was the last of the beeches, a

70-foot-long smooth trunk, shining a glacé silver under the sun, waiting to be 'tushed' away to the lorry.

The felling of the beeches was part of another pattern, the pattern of denudation – and erosion, retribution for the rapine committed by man for quick profits. I knew the man who owned this land. While prices were high he was cutting every tree that would sell. He was not replanting. During the two world wars in Britain alone nearly two million acres of woodland had been levelled. A little while before I had looked with horror at a photograph of a mountain of logs beside which stood the dwarfed figure of a man. That mountain measured the size of my own guilt, for it was the amount of wood – the harvest from 24 acres of forest – needed to supply the newsprint for one edition of an American paper. It was a sight to check the hand of any man who writes, to make him assess the value of the words he sets on paper.

I went on and the sunlight seemed a little dimmer. Beyond Bury and its rectory gate made of welded-together axe, scythe, pitchfork and spade, the lane unwound towards the nearing bluffs of the Beacon hills. In the glazed air winger gnats made misty whorls. Flocks of chaffinches were feeding in the beech hedges, and as they scattered ahead with volleys of twitters I caught glimpses of the white rumps of bramblings, winter visitors from the birth plantations of Scandinavia. A band of redwings flew across the road from a field full of root-tops, and the songs of robins and dunnocks struck my ears in short, sudden bursts.

As I had done before, I left the car and climbed the path, a piece of white tape where feet had worn the thin skin of the turf from the underlying chalk, to the rounded tip of the Beacon. And, as before, I thought of Richard Jefferies walking on his beloved downs above Swindon. 'The very light of the sun was whiter and more brilliant there.' The purity of the air which washed me in billowing invisible waves, the perfection of design of the Vale, which ran from here into the Midlands, with its intricacies of rivers and hedgerows and meadows and coppices, all tiny integral parts of the whole that was agricultural England, gave me a profound and curiously possessive pleasure. The low-slung sun was warm and a lark was singing far away with a tinkling quality that made me think of Andrew's toy xylophone. I lay for a time with closed eyes feeling the sun reddening my eyelids and touching the bristly fleshiness of the grass with my fingers. The sensation was a combination of the elemental and the abstract; both at once; a pantheist flowing away into, and commingling with the atmosphere, and a solid, earth-rooted firmness and security: harmony and balance.

Soon I went on. The reservoirs were not far away now. I came down the hill, through the slopped about outskirts of the town, and turned on to the narrow road that cut between the two lakes. It seemed a long time since I had been there. Again I felt dismal surprise at the squalor of suburban building and no-man's-land agriculture that characterized the district, a dislike that was always glossed over in memory by the vision of the great congresses of duck and waders which ignored the brick tide drawing always nearer, and flighted down still from autumn and winter skies.

On the smallest of the three canal reservoirs four mute swans were floating. The stillness and serenity of the water, the blinding veins of sunshine, the floating swans all made a design of heraldic formality. Beyond, in the middle distance, was a dark lozenge upon the water, duck. I began to walk around the edge nearer to them and to get the sun at my back. In the rough jumble of grass below the bank was a pustule of red, and looking closer I saw that already in bloom was the dead-nettle, the Saxon *deffe-nettil*, descriptive of the impotence of the stingless heart-shaped leaves. The drab little red flowers were a posy on winter's grave.

Here at these reservoirs the bittern had nested in the last century, and at odd intervals the bittern's boom could still be heard in winters and early springs – here, only thirty miles from London. Here, during the war, an osprey stayed for a few days to hunt. Here the three varieties of diver – great northern, black-throated and red-throated – were regularly seen. Here the great crested grebe had bred frequently since 1918. And to here in 1938, when one of the lakes had been drained to fill the canal, came two little ringed plovers to nest for the first known time in Britain, so beginning a colonization drive that was still in progress. It was that occurrence that moved me to write the little ringed plover's story, thereby encountering suspicion and resentment among the amateur scientific ornithologists who did not welcome the attention of a writer. But it was a thrilling and fascinating story, and I went ahead and learned the facts from watching the birds myself so that the published records should have for me a virility of meaning.

Now the little ringed plovers were thousands of miles away in Equatorial Africa. Despite the zealousness of the sun it was still winter; the winter legions of duck were still here. I was much nearer then than now and the lowering sun was directly behind, so that the floating masses were picked out in pure line and colour. Without the glasses I could see that most were mallard and that among them were teal and wigeon. As I squatted to give my binoculars steadiness, a *spring* of ten teal came slanting in. They flew with the velocity of waders and as they dropped upon the widespread gathering they did a smart kicking turn that brought them skidding past me. I could see the red green-blobbed heads of the drakes and the chalk slashes down their backs. They watered, making furrows of foam, the coulters of their webbed feet slicing seams of water, the mouldboards of their breasts heaving the seams over. Even as the teal settled, a group of mallard went beating off with a grunting of wings that over-rode the broken piping of the swimming teal. Before the water had ceased to vibrate to their landing, the new flock took off again, quacking harrassedly. The alarm spread in a thin weaving trail through the assembly, and almost simultaneously from a dozen different points small parties broke away until only a small black core was left: a pack of coots which drowsed in sullen indifference to my presence.

The sky was slashed by duck. The splinter groups crossed and recrossed in a vast diagram. They made sharp incisions upon the blurry yellow of the sun and whirred across high and dark. The sound of the passing wings was like wind in the tree tops heard from within a wood.

There was no advantage in concealment now. I stepped through the elder brush and out on to the bumpy mattress of dried-up marsh, where dead reeds were like crumpled balls of yellow parchment. Two more mallards got up from where they had been skulking in the cover of the reeds, and almost on their tails rose a smaller bird that was a flickering black and white as it sped up at a sharp angle, a green sandpiper. I watched the sandpiper towering high in the planished blue sky where cirrus cloud was like steam rising from hot hammered metal.

I walked on slowly, following the erratic line of the shore, with a sense of fragile pleasure. It was like stealing, for myself alone, a day from April. My eyes stroked the bright perfection of the afternoon like a miser fingering coins. It was not a completed happiness. Little tentacles of thoughts vigorously pushed their way into the calm, trying to choke it, overpower it with their priggish reminders. On my desk was a half-done chapter, begun without enthusiasm, petering off into a negation of disgust; there were letters to write, an article to retype and send away; Bee was again saddled with the children, trying to find time after feeding the baby to give half an hour to the house accounts; there was the crescent of unkempt grass before the rookery beeches that I had promised to autoscythe. There were a dozen community things clamouring for attention, and as many private things, and here I was wandering irresponsibly beside the reservoirs, lingering to let the sharp graphite flight of duck engrave itself on my mind, hearing guiltily the rasp of the reeds against my shoes, the twittering of the teal-flocks, and the sentimentalizing of a robin over its rubbishy haunt. The guilt grew bigger until I could ward it off no longer. It forced in and took possession, standing like a bailiff, arms folded, loweringly bullying.

I walked on. I wasn't going to turn back. I would circle the lake and return to the road along the opposite bank. The flutterings of release had stopped; I was back on the ground. It became more and more difficult to wrestle free of the entanglements of every day, I thought irritably, and at moments such as this it seemed that joining the community had increased, not lessened, the number of entanglements.

A carrion crow tramped through the air with something in its bill. I strained my eyes to see what it was and thought I could make out the swinging thread of a rat's tail. The crow spotted me and slanted sluggishly away, behind the wood.

I tried to remember when the process had started. Boyhood seemed now to have been the distillation of freedom. I tried to reconstruct the sensation of treading lightly across the Park on a spring day – it was always spring, the sunlight smeared like butter upon the fields; rooks jostling and clearing their throats in the faint heights of the Lower Lake Wood; bluebells like leaks from the swimming blue of the sky; the crispness of a new nest; the luminous dizziness from watching kestrels soaring above their dead tree – but I could not. It was there in my memory, but with the bright transparency of a bubble. And when I tried to grasp it, it slid buoyantly away. Then, surely, there had been completion, an immersion in the day and the hour? . . . But, no, it was probably a nostalgic fancy. The doubts and fears and worries had been as real and as insinuating then as now. Different worries, the hatred for a master, the terror of an examination, the lust for an air pistol, the raw shyness of childhood, but just as large, just as persistent. No, the womb was the last stockade; after that it was a running fight through unknown territory.

When I got back to the road the sun was a red balloon settling tremblingly upon the earth. The illusion of a spring day had gone like other illusions. A surly winter dusk was thrusting in. The air was tart on my face and as I climbed the bank towards my car there blew a wind that tweaked the lobes of my ears. More duck were coming in with the night. First I heard the swish of their wings and then I saw swift blackness of flocks manoeuvreing down to the lakes, and a little later there was a muffled hiss of split water and the mutter of their voices.

I did not raise the hood for that would have ended the day there. For a moment I hesitated, because it would have been pleasant to shut myself in the box of canvas and celluloid, but I drove off into the quickening river of biting darkness, watching my headlights go bumping their way along the grass-banked road, frozen by the rushing wind into a solid numbness that had a warm safe core.

Chapter Eleven

I enjoyed being a barrow-boy. When Alec first asked me if I would like to take a turn on the market stall I was dubious, chiefly because of my shaky mental arithmetic. I found, however, that I could work my way through a calculation to an approximately correct result (deciding in favour of the customer if any doubt remained) while deftly swinging round a bag of apples or tying flowers with raffia.

The starting of the stall was part of the battle against insolvency. Alec had been the instigator and organizer. Each Saturday morning I paraded with my car, Ian or Christopher with his, and Hilary Gardener (that wasn't her name; she was the gardener, as distinct from Hilary Harper) with Gerald and John's photography van, at the greenhouses. There we loaded up with produce, tomatoes, lettuces, cucumbers, leeks, but chiefly flowers. We grew magnificent gladioli and chrysanthemums, and our potted azalias became a feature of Boxwood Saturday market.

Here an account should be given of the important function of the horticultural society in Berewode's economy. It had been officially founded a year or so after the start of the community, but it had had an uneven and unsuccessful childhood. Baxter, who lived with his family in the north-side cottage and who had been head gardener to the previous occupier, was the society's mainstay. There, too, worked Basil Hobson on a part-time paid basis. The enormous amount of labour put in by Alec was done only for the satisfaction of seeing the grounds gradually reclaimed. At one juncture there had been a Land Girl, and a variety of community women and villagers from time to time earned their two shillings an hour in the gardens. It was recognized as a scandal that the gardens should be a liability instead of the precious asset they so clearly could be, but it was not until a crisis period just before we arrived that positive measures were taken. A new committee was set up and given complete freedom of action to put the gardens on a paying footing. At that time the society's debt amounted to £555. The soil was in poor condition, showing a lime deficiency and a lack of manure. There were wide gaps in flower production, several types were rapidly becoming obsolete, and some already were. Plots were being left unused, except by weeds. There was no efficient system for marketing the produce surplus to the house's needs.

The first moves made were the building up of tons of compost for use in the spring: the hen-house manure was collected methodically instead of being wasted as before, and all the rottable refuse from the house was directed from the dustbins to the compost heaps. Leaf mould was harvested from the Long Wood and carted to the greenhouses; turves were bought for potting. Two strips of ground – the garden of the derelict cottage and the surrounds of the old piggery – were reclaimed. New frames were built. The fruit-cage was swooped upon and cleared of diseased, aged blackcurrants. Four hundred new cuttings, gooseberry and raspberry, were planted. The strawberry beds were doubled in size. A part of the overgrown Italian garden was dug over and planted with gladioli, while Alec put down annuals in the piggery strip. An outlay was made for bulbs, azaleas, geraniums, scabious plants and carnations.

While all these preparations were being made the object – a steadily absorbing market – had to be found. Again it was Alec who persuaded a well-known London vegetarian restaurant and fruiterers to take small supplies, which quickly increased when the quality of Bereworde produce was seen. In the first three months just under £100 worth of produce was taken up to the greengrocery in the dicky of Christopher's car.

The stall in Boxwood market was used as a subsidiary channel. Here blooms too poor for the London shop, or those that would not last over the weekend, could be sold. The first ten Saturday morning stalls earned the community £76.

Stall duty could be tedious on wet or cold days when Hilary and I huddled under the tarpaulin, bored and melancholy, watching people hurrying past on essential shopping. But in summer, and more especially in spring when people were eager to be reminded by a bowl of primroses on the sideboard that the sun was arcing higher in the sky, then it was pleasant. I liked the meandering tides of people, and the presence of the other stalls, the ice-cream barrow, the 'jewellery' stall run by two chokered cockneys from Tottenham, the stall piled with antique radios, chipped ornate clocks and a miscellany of secondhand clothes.

My friend David Malbert, down from London for the weekend, was disappointed when he found his way to the stall from the station to come upon me propped against a post whiling away a dull morning by reading Sartre's *What Is Literature?* It was out of character, he said, and he seemed to think it was rather funny. I reminded him that Mary Webb had earned her living while writing her books by running a greengrocery stall.

On a Saturday in the middle of February John suggested at breakfast that as the stock of wood was running low I should take time off from the stall and join him on the sawbench. That suited me very well, for the stall duty had fallen into too steady a routine. Hilary said she could manage by herself, so I got my gauntlets from the car and hailed John. We worked fast for we wanted to clear away the pile of branches and wedge-split trunk, the winnings from the oak that had been thrown in the lodge copse weeks ago. By twelve my left arm ached from exerting pressure on the different shaped and sized balks that John slid on to the steel tray, from pressing each one forward evenly so that the spinning 24-inch blade sliced through cleanly; my throat and nostrils were clogged with the fine dust that sprayed high and even got beneath the ARP anti-gas cellulose goggles I wore; my ears were deadened by the ceaseless harsh hum which rose to a howl as the teeth tore through the fibre of the wood, leaving at each end a smooth disc upon which the annual rings made soft circular patterns of cream, fawn and ruddy brown.

We rolled the bench back into the workshop and walked to the Plumes for a beer. It was St Valentine's Day, the day on which traditionally birds choose their mates. It is difficult to see how this can ever have been regarded as more than a picturesque tale. No countryman with his eyes open can ever have believed it. The rooks, of course, were lingering longer in the pines and beeches at the front of the house, ferreting about in the gale-damaged nests, tentatively pulling them into shape. The partridges, too, were disbanding their coveys. The day before I had seen half a dozen, four cocks and two hens, I judged, in a melee in a field of autumn-sown oats. But they were preliminary gestures. The conduct of winter still guided the birds, and the loose flocks of redwings that bolted from the hedges as we approached, the garrulous house sparrow flocks and immigrant greenfinches in the stackyard of Berry Farm, were evidence of the fallibility of the tradition.

After a pint of beer I left John at the Plumes, talking to one of the villagers who helped in the garden, for I felt like a walk. I re-entered the grounds by the west gate, following the path past the ivy-mounded wall of the Italian garden, with its seventeenth-century Florentian wrought-iron gate, now sadly rusted, and along the edge of the common meadow. On the Ordnance Survey map this ground was still shown as part of Estodham Common and marked with little hairy half circles denoting furze. The war had changed that. Under the direction of the local Agricultural Executive Committee the snub nose of land, bounded by the two lanes that met in a junction at the square tip, had been ploughed up. All that was left as indication of what it had once been was a crescent-shaped sector, almost in the middle, that had defeated the tractor, now an atoll tufted with gold-flowered gorse, and a deep little dell near the western hedge abrim with thorns, where magpies still nested.

Now the place where linnets and red-backed shrike had once hidden their nests in dense spiny cover was naked, hacked into the shape and character of land that would produce a little of the food Britain needed. The field was in furrow, weathering until a spell of dry weather or frost would reduce the two inches of top soil to a friable condition. Then the disc harrow would be driven out to form a tilth, to be followed by harrows and drill, until the spring-corn seed bed was ready.

Half a dozen goldfinches were plundering the thistles and wizened stalks of rose-bay willow herb that cluttered the broad margin between the walled kitchen garden and the track. Their flight away was like the fluttering of small flames upon the air. Just ahead was a thick brush of Douglas firs and young sycamores, with a few bird cherries forcing doggedly through. On the clearer ground in front straddled some limes, a few silver firs, a clannish group of Scots pines, a feathery ash and several beeches. The tallest trees of the group were the pines, whose long, lean trunks glowed salmon in the morning sun, and the beeches which towered like colonnades of smoothest grey stone.

Yet when I looked from the children's bedroom, as I often did to watch the rooks at their nests or grey squirrels swinging across their branch trapezes, I saw two trees that jutted high above the pines and beeches, rearing like green mountain peaks above their foothills. They were suggestive of aggressive power and immensity that was oddly alien amid the modest, moderate English growth.

Little wonder, for these giants were *sequoia gigantia*, redwoods, the 'big trees' of the Sierra Nevada, the greatest trees on earth, which in the Californian mountains swell over 30 foot in diameter and project upwards 300 foot and more. Driving their octopus roots into the chalky marl of the escarpment, these two foreigners had already reached 150 foot in height. To do that had taken them less than a century. More than likely they were planted in the early 1850s, when transplants were shipped across and sold in British nurseries for £5 each. In this country they still bear the name wellingtonia, bestowed in commemoration of the Duke of Wellington.

The redwood is an evergreen. Now, with the rookery trees thin with winter, the redwoods loomed against the granite sky like immense dusky-green lupins. Earlier, before I had even begun thinking of the coming spring, I had noticed that the redwoods were blooming. Their clustered flowers had showered an orange pollen which, from a distance, looked like patches of sunlight that had magically spread upon the hard bare earth from a cloud-blocked sky. I knew that the cones would not appear until summer was at its height, tiny silver nodules that over a year later would spray forth their millions of seeds. Most, of course, would never find hold, for when a shoot did struggle through it would almost certainly be killed by squirrels and rabbits crunching away the tender tip.

The redwoods were attractive to the winter gangs of tits that hunted through the spinney, for their rugged, fissured trunks were populated with insects liked by the tits, and the cones were broken open for their flesh. Twice I had seen goldcrests, miniature birds with splinters of fire on their olive skulls, feeding on the heavy bough fans, and jays used the redwoods as look-out posts; there could have been none better.

It was partly for that reason – that they drew bird-life to themselves – that I often thrust through the bramble thickets, like wartime barbed-wire defences, and walked around the redwoods; but only partly for that reason. In their own right the redwoods fascinated me. They had a personal grandeur and majesty of a sort that belonged to no other neighbouring tree, a sombre individuality that sent them up to that altitude where they lived in loneliness, far aloft the springtime racket of the rook-tenement, high above the packed suburban cheek-by-jowl intimacy of the overgrown little wood.

I was about to strike off to look at the redwoods when I heard John shouting from behind: 'Come on, we'd better finish that pile.'

Slightly irritated and once again vaguely resentful of the way Bereworde seemed always to control and divert one's casual inclinations, I turned back and walked with John into the yard. With a pause for lunch we worked on the bench until my head was dizzy with the noise, my chest raw with wood-dust. It was late afternoon when the last chunks were thrown into the rotunda. Stiff and oddly flat in spirits, I tramped upstairs to wash. I felt I wanted to breathe some fresh air before supper. I whistled Bambi and strolled along the gravel forecourt. Suddenly the dog went spearing off into the dusk and a second or two later I heard the hysterical yapping that meant she had seen a rabbit to which she would give desperate chase and never catch.

I stood for exasperated seconds listening to the terrier's yaps moving deeper into the spinney, then I turned off the path and followed. I had no wish to go any farther because my body was still stiff and aching, but I followed because the dog had a reckless habit of hurling herself down rabbit holes and scrambling forward into the moist darkness. I was afraid that one day one would be her grave.

Branches to which wet, dead leaves still clung miserably smacked my face and the clogged mat of decayed nettles, willow herb and bracken tripped my feet. The sound of furious scratching led me to Bambi. She was beside one of the redwoods, half out of sight down a burrow and shooting the fawn earth out beyond her plastered hind quarters. She came out to my whistle and with an insane and impotent hunting fever in her eyes.

As I turned to go back I looked through the cage of dipping boughs up the redwood's vast bulk, but there was not a movement of birds: everywhere in the fading light there was the complete silence of dead things. A blotch of white on the side of the trunk caught my eye, and I dipped in to look closer. That was an odd thing. The splash of white droppings was just below a tiny cavity, an alcove oval in shape hollowed into the sheer cliff of the trunk. Obviously it was the roosting place of a bird and equally obviously it had been dug out by a beak.

The hole puzzled me. I had never before come upon a similar one. Woodpecker, had been the thought that had instantly flashed into my brain, but it was rejected as quickly. Compared with the drilling of a woodpecker this clumsy little indentation (it was no more) was an amateur's work. Very well, but what could it be?

For some minutes I stood motionless, half hoping to see the unknown bird come flittering in through the dusk to its roosting cave. Nothing happened, and there was an utter stillness; in the smeary light the shadow of the redwood stretched up and up, apparently endlessly, into the hidden sky. With the dog slouching at my heels, now sulky with defeat and exhaustion, I pushed on through the wood. Soon I could see the lights in the house and hear the laughter of Andrew and Amanda in the bathroom, and the little mystery was forgotten in the joyous welcome, given wetly and impulsively after so brief an absence.

Yet the dissatisfaction of ignorance remained and two days later I went deliberately to the redwood. It was twilight again. I circled on to the tree across the one-time common so that if the bird was there I would come flat upon it. I trod quietly through the fallen fern and edged into the screen of tufty branches. As my eyes were seeking the spot there was a light scurry and the escape of a small form – and, yes, it had come from the alcove! . . . But what it was I couldn't tell: there was only a blurred impression of a small dark winged shape.

Now I was determined to solve the problem. Two hours later I left the house again and I carried a torch. It was quite dark, moonless, and the air had the clamminess of incipient rain. A tawny owl was crying in the Long Wood and rabbits leaped away between the beeches as I crossed to the spinney. Black as the night was I could see the huge silhouettes of the two redwoods like twin spires above the general tree line.

I followed the same route, across the corner of the old common, and softly stepped beneath the great tree's canopy. The ray stabbed out, faltered and then focused on the place. In the alcove was a bird, and as I pushed the light nearer I saw by its white-streaked brown back, its silver breast and its thin curved bill that it was a treecreeper. It was bemused by the glare and it did no more than shift its wings and turn its head in a dazed fashion. I put out my hand to touch it, then stopped an inch away and quietly withdrew, not switching off the light until I was out of the tree's perimeter.

Afterwards I made enquiries. Yes, it had recently been observed in a few places that treecreepers excavated themselves holes in redwoods — but, it seemed, only in redwoods, whose bark was soft enough for their beaks. It was a classic example of how birds learn, adjust themselves to new conditions. Yet there was more to it than that. What had captured my imagination was the thought of that treecreeper, a bird only twice the length of my index finger, sleeping secure through the bitter winter nights in the fortress of the biggest tree of all, the redwood.

Chapter Twelve

After spending several weekends with us my friend John Knight said to me: 'Whenever I come down here I always start by hating Bereworde. And then when it's time to return to London I hate going.'

In a less extreme way those two emotions ran concurrently through my time there. Two forces were at work within me constantly, one the attraction towards the communal idea, the other, like the pull of gravity, away from it to the isolation and self-containment essential to me as a writer. The explanation was, I decided, that ideally the communal man should be a man of action, an extrovert whose energies are poured unstintingly into the common pool. As the months passed I saw more and more clearly that Ian's concept of Bereworde was beyond practical realization by imperfect humans such as we. His was a rounded stylized picture, like one of those panoramic picture maps in which all aspects of a village's life used to be portrayed – leisure represented by the youth idling on the river bank, work by haymakers in a field. That was his private vision and he conscientiously fitted his own conduct to it. He took on far more than he could manage, and usually managed it. Somehow, and I never understood quite how, he found it possible to run his business, nurse his constituency, and contribute more than his share to the communal work. His weekends were a kaleidoscopic switch from one activity to another. On a Sunday morning he would be cross-sawing a tree in the Long Wood, cleaning out the chicken run a little later. During lunch he would be sub-editing the draft of a speech, in the afternoon in his study in the old farm buildings preparing a brief for a court case the next day. After helping Anna with the children's teas, he would be off in his MG to a committee meeting in Downsteeple. He might get back in time for a horticultural society discussion or in time to produce a bottle of sherry and act as host at an emergency party. Sometimes, late at night, when one would encounter him just as he had returned home, duffel-coated, tousel-haired, cutting himself a cheese sandwich in the kitchen, he looked haggard to a point of collapse, and one felt that sooner or later there would come a sudden breakdown. But it never happened. Always, in the final resort, he seemed able to turn on the tap of yet another inner tank of energy. Anna, too, in a different way, flourished on this erratic, last-minute, disorganized existence. She could always find time to give help in the grounds or talk to someone who was in a depression.

I admired their unselfishness, their natural universality of feeling, and envied them their stamina, but it was a state of affairs that nevertheless awoke a disquiet, a horror, almost, in me. The Parfitts made themselves common property in a grand manner; 98 per cent of themselves was at the disposal of the community. My percentage was much lower. The difficulty was that they set a dizzy standard for anyone of less heroic proportions. For instance, I can imagine few women rising so gallantly and cheerfully to the situation Bee put herself in by going into labour during the festivities of the following – and last – Christmas at Bereworde. In the early hours of the day after Boxing Day, when the current party was still going full blast (or rather the party that had started on Christmas Eve, for individual parties had become blurred into a single long one of fluctuating animation), Bee decided that the ambulance had better be called. Anna took charge. She sat up with Bee until the ambulance arrived at 4.30 a.m., and then climbed in and rode with her on the forty miles to London. She stayed in the hospital all the next morning, went off and had two or three hours' sleep at a friend's flat, returned to the hospital, and eventually arrived back at Bereworde late that evening to start all her own domestic duties.

That sort of thing, a readiness to help when it was much more convenient personally to side-step out of the picture, was perhaps the best characteristic of the community. It varied with individuals, and there were a few who lacked the virtue altogether, but typical of the way the community rallied round was the time in our second summer there when Bee and I, on our way on the first stage of a journey to

Hungary – part journalism, part holiday – were involved in a car smash. Mine, fortunately as it was loaded with among other things two children, stayed upright, while the other car somersaulted several times. A telephone call to Bereworde brought down a rescue squad. Bee and the children were driven to London. Another car took me first into Downsteeple, then back to the house. Telephone calls were made for me. And later that day a car took me up to London to rejoin Bee.

And always at the front in such situations were the Parfitts. Nevertheless, their casual, make-shift, improvising attitude to life was at times disconcerting and occasionally maddening. Ian would make an arrangement to do something and completely forget about it until five minutes before it was due to happen, if at all. There was the outstanding case of the New Zealanders. One week when the Parfitts were away a mysterious telegram came. 'Arriving Saturday,' it stated, and was signed 'Harvey'. No-one knew anything of any Harvey and after some desultory and inconclusive enquiries the telegram was put on someone's mantelshelf and forgotten. At lunchtime on Saturday there was a rumble of wheels on the gravel and a hire-car drew up outside the front door. From it got a man, a woman and four children. Beside them were placed a trunk and many suitcases. The man walked into the hall. Several of us were standing around looking at each other a trifle nervously. 'Is Ian Parfitt here?' the man asked. 'My name's Harvey.'

In degrees the story was pieced together, starting from the startling fact that the Harveys had arrived from New Zealand with their four children to live at Bereworde for an indefinite time. It appeared that over a year before Harvey had come upon one of the community's advertisements in a magazine. He had written to say that at some time in the future he and his family were coming to settle in Britain and suggested that, as the ideals and political complexion of the community approximated so closely to his own, they might join. Ian had replied in a typical Ian manner. Without pointing out that it was impossible to say precisely what accommodation might be available so far ahead, he had thrown out an open-arm invitation, surrounded by political reflection and wittily-worded description of life at Bereworde, declaring unequivocally that the Harveys could regard Bereworde as their first, and, if they liked, permanent, English home. One or two people vaguely remembered Ian mentioning this correspondence at some far away family meeting, but in view of its nebulousness it had not been looked upon as a commitment. Since then, it appeared, Harvey had written two more letters to Ian. His last had been answered three or four months ago – a brief, friendly note re-asserting his promise of hospitality. Now the Harveys had come, with every trapping of permanent establishment.

This was all very fine, but there was one grave obstacle: there was no room. Bereworde had its full complement of families. Diplomatically this was explained to the Harveys, who, all things considered, took it bravely, although Mrs Harvey, who up to then had remained silent, with an expression of deepening anguish as the truth was gradually filtered through to them, exclaimed anxiously: 'But where are we going to sleep *tonight*?'

No one could give a clear-cut answer to that question. It was covertly decided that Ian really would have to handle this one. The Harveys were brought in, food was found for them, and they were vigorously entertained until tea-time when Ian and Anna returned home.

There may have been a fleeting frown of worry across Ian's brow when he was brought face to face with the unexpected guests, but it was no more than fleeting. His customary eager smile wiped it off and he advanced, hand outstretched, with every sign of pleasure.

'My memory,' he grinned. 'It's quite appalling. I really am dreadfully sorry if this has caused you any upset, but don't you worry. We'll fit you in. Delighted to have you. Hope you'll stay on here once you've seen the community in action.'

It seemed to me that that was ingenious improvization, that for ten minutes or so Ian was fighting hard exactly to place the Harveys, to remember who they were, where they had come from, what they were doing here. But he allowed none of his perplexity to leak through to embarrass the Harveys. Anna, who had risen as charmingly and skilfully to the delicate crisis, bustled round. That night and for several more nights the Harveys slept in the Parfitt's room, while they used a shake-down in one of the stables. There was an extraordinary family meeting called and it was decided that it would be possible by co-operative contribution to fit out for the Harveys a room used for storing junk. This was done. The fact that the Harveys stayed only a fortnight, when they left for some remote provincial town where

Mr Harvey had found a job, may have been due to a suspicion that they were an unplanned addition to the community.

Another similar incident, which, although not due in any way to the Parfitt's memory lapses, was symptomatic of Berewordean life, was when a kitchen maid, a dull, mangold-like girl with an illegitimate child, arrived back uninvited two months after she had quit her job. It was a simple situation: she had been sacked from the milk bar where she had gone to work, had nowhere to go, so had returned. The community neither wanted nor needed her. She was a slatternly and lazy girl. Our finances were then at barrel-scraping depth, with nothing left over for extra staff. But, as always happened, the community's better nature prevailed. The girl was taken in, a cot rounded up for the child, and she was re-established in the kitchen, which quickly deteriorated in cleanliness.

Indeed it may have been this sort of unpredictable, harrassing occurrence that added a piquancy to community life. There was always an element of adventure about the, outwardly, most commonplace routines. The daily business of getting up, eating breakfast and driving to the station for the London train seemed always to be charged with tantalizing uncertainty. The gap between Bereworde and the eight miles' distant station was bridged in a variety of ways during the community's existence. At first, there was a contract with the village shop-owner, who arrived each morning at eight o'clock in an enormous, decrepit Hispano Suiza equipped with speaking tube and horsehair seats. Theoretically, the car sounded its sonorous and lowing horn as it drew to a standstill at the front door, the menfolk trooped out, took their seats and were driven at comfortable speed to catch the eight-thirty. Daily theory was farcically betrayed by practice. What happened was that when the car's horn boomed through the house, the dining-room was occupied by two men of orderly and responsible character, Alec Cameron and Jim Stubbs. They sat over the last cup of tea and cigarette, with glum and cynically resigned expressions awaiting the usual pandemonium. This was made up of violent shoe-crashings on the stairs, the bursting in of Aubrey, Ian, Chris, myself, and any irregular travellers, perhaps Anna or Ruthene who were going to spend the day in London, in different stages of undress and unpreparedness. At these times Aubrey's volatile temperament snapped its leash. There was a catherine wheel of action in which he was the wildly gyrating core. Toast was grabbed, cups of tea slopped out, yelling children quieted by pleading shouts, last-second instructions bawled to wives, briefcases snatched, and, in explosive and spasmodic bounds, the car was filled. Invariably last was Ian, scurrying down the steps as the car was rocking away, tie in one hand, marmaladed toast in the other. By that time it was anything up to ten minutes past eight and there followed a hair-raising charge down eight miles of lane and country road to the station.

Later, when the community's bank would no longer stand for the taxi contract, the journey was made piecemeal in any car or cars which were in working order. Often John drove us down in Gerald's Lea Francis, six or seven of us crammed in the flimsy, hoodless framework, screeching at sixty miles an hour through the rain of winter mornings, John at the wheel in pyjamas and dressing gown, his heavy, dark face thunderous with pre-breakfast gloom, his carpeted foot rammed down on the accelerator.

The inescapable fact was that the community was, in some of its aspects, bizarre. This was a point that no newspaper ever neglected to stress. For, in its time, Bereworde was exploited by many of the national papers as a source for what news editors call a 'crazy story'. At fairly regular intervals a taxi would draw up and disgorge a reporter and a cameraman. As is the schizophrenic habit of newspaper people, the reporter, who was often a woman, would be charming, intelligent and obviously genuinely interested in the objects and achievements of the experiment: and then would make for the nearest telephone and dictate to the office the customary distorted, angled, fever-coloured stunt story about Bereworde and its curious cranks. The only balanced and sensibly-written account was the photographic feature published by *Picture Post* and written by Hilde Marchant in the days before I came to know and like her as a colleague and respect her as a fine journalist.

I suspect that it was this out-of-the-ordinariness that was one of its attractions for me. I frankly enjoyed the sensation of taking part in a trial run of this kind and the knowledge that probably some of the community's hard-earned experience might in indistinctly indirect ways be of benefit to other people at some unspecifiable time ahead. In fact, without searching too hard for morals, I believe that my two years there did transform me into a little more of a social being, did make me a little more flexible in social give and take, and I think it was Ian's example – which was never flaunted in a holier-than-thou spirit – which made whatever difference there is in me today. Nevertheless, in the midst of this sort of reflection about the community days I always find it necessary to analyze the apparent virtues for their inherent vices. The toleration and understanding – 'to the point of compassion' – about which Ian spoke sincerely at the depressing family meeting in our first autumn there, were certainly things he practised in a routine, workaday way. Yet sometimes they slipped over the edge into foolishness. The tough, teeth-cracking kernel (which gathered so many ideological layers) of the cause of the community's ultimate dissolution was financial. It need not have been such a teeth-cracker of a problem if Ian had been less tolerant with certain individuals who had no scruples about using the community as a cross between a free lodging-house and a disembodied money-lender. I have no sure idea what the total of money owing to him personally was when the reckoning day came, but I do know that unpaid rents added up to several hundreds of pounds. And the bitterish residue that remained was the squalid and not unfamiliar injustice that the ones who acted worst were most favourably placed at the end. Those of us who accepted our share of the disaster, and that was nearly everyone, found themselves in desperately unpleasant situations when it came to finding the necessary money for somewhere else to live.

But that is an anticipation. Not until the sad tail-end did those unattractive spectres start stalking about openly. They had to lurk well in the background in the face of the hectic, spirited and vital life that crackled through Bereworde like an electric current, giving the old house a galvanization that, I'm certain, it never felt before or since.

Chapter Thirteen

Meanwhile spring had sidled in slyly behind our backs: as it usually does. One morning the car started without having to be rolled down Pedler's Hill; on the way along the drive my sleep-bleared consciousness was suddenly driven through by pulses of yellow, yellow of primroses beneath the beeches and of wind-fluttered daffodils around the lodge shrubberies; my hand did not turn rigid with cold on the throttle; and while waiting for the eight-thirty I heard the ringing *keekeekeekee* of a wryneck coming from the house-ringed plot of copse and field across the line.

The next day was a Saturday, April's first. I excused myself from stall-duty, and, buckling my leg tight, walked out to catch up on all that had been happening. My leg was swinging smoothly, the steel cup held securely to the stump, and I walked rapidly past Clementine Farm and the row of plain brick cottages whose gardens mixed cabbages and flowers with the practical design of the labourer's garden, along past the pillows of furze that spluttered with flames of blossom (as they had been doing even on Christmas Day) and the young rods of bracken that looked sweet enough to crunch like celery, and along beside the strictly cropped thorn hedges that were still branch trellis, long, black typographical lines, except where a blackthorn made an ornamental initial letter from new pale flowers. Not far in front was the start of the great Buckwood Estate, there where woods ran like coastal cliffs from one compass point of my eyesight to its extreme. I had been in the woods only once before, at Christmas time to steal moss for the horticultural society who had got an order for wreaths from their London store. Then they had been black-green silent with winter, like the interior of a Mendip cavern, mud and wet trunks and a feeling of lasting defeat. As I approached now I tried to describe to myself the reasons for a palpable difference. I could not put it down to a renewal of the summer prospect of leaves, for leaves had not yet shifted the emphasis from bare bark to themselves; nor had this adolescent sun the mature power to spread that May butter light upon the land. There was no obvious illusion, because there was the land, as hard-jawed, almost, as it had been two months ago, and even if three chaffinches were singing their spring songs it was a sound no more significant in itself than a thrush's January impatience. Yet I was aware of a chain reaction, a series of retorts that were changing my mood from expectancy into a sharp, heightened emotional awareness of being actually in the presence of spring. It was a sensation that had become dimmer as I had grown older. Since I had passed the age of twenty, I had been able to look back with shrewdly clear sight upon the curious sublimity that had saturated me as a bird-nesting boy. I found it an odd experience, this looking back with sophisticated eyes at juvenile mysticism, like staring at an Ordnance Survey map of a district one has never been to: there in fine and meticulous detail are the contours and the bridle roads and the unfenced deciduous woods; the intimate facts of the place are laid out in cold, accurate completeness; and yet it tells you nothing. So it was with my examination of my 15-year-old self, a diagram on feeling. As my understanding of the boy who was nostalgic for the things he was seeing for the first time, who had caressed a tree, who had wept for the joy that was a blade in his breast as he listened to reed warblers on the Upper Lake, grew larger, so in proportion did my ability to experience those feelings lessen. It was not that I wanted to remain in a state of religious mania, but it saddened me when, so often, I found myself surrounded by the influences that once would have produced a confusion of ecstasy, and to feel little or nothing. I moved through them insulated by a cold layer of practicality; there were too many years, too much experience between me and them. Now and then I caught a flash of the old magic, like the momentary brilliant flourish of a conjurer's silk scarf; shortly I was in contact with what I had once known. It was half true when I told people who believed me to be a Nature Lover: 'I no longer care deeply for the countryside.' As I got nearer to the mass of

Buckwood woods I suddenly remembered a scene — driving with my father along a Buckinghamshire lane not far from where we lived and hearing him tell my mother that a business associate was going to build a housing estate there. I remembered with sudden vividness, so vivid that I almost *felt* the anger again, my savage indignation. I had shouted at my father and been rebuked, and tears and sulking followed, but it had been a passion too stormy to control. The thought that a single brick should efface a few inches of that hillside where a young beech wood slanted, where a jay was calling, was not to be borne. I had to cry out against it. In the same way I hated, with an actually personal hatred, anyone I saw intruding in my beloved parkland. Now no angry sob would arise for a murdered hawk: all that was left was a sense of distaste for game preserving in general and a diluted regret that the hawk was dead: it was the adulteration of the spontaneous and pure thought of childhood.

The memory of those unhappy few minutes of fifteen years before set up a stronger radiation towards those unreachable years than I had known for a long time. I skin stripped. It was as if I had regrown insect antennae that flickered with nervous sensitivity against the texture of the April morning. A wide ride struck direct into the thickness of the woods and I turned in without thinking about it; it was as insistent as a spoken invitation. Mostly the wood was of young oak and ash, and, here and there, a sallow bush yellowing with blossom. I seemed simultaneously to be hearing and seeing a thousand fresh things. With conscious joy I separated the threads of sound that were weaving together into a concert of bird music. Singing all at once were chiffchaff (the first of the year), great tit, yellowhammer, woodpigeon, chaffinch, blackbird and mistle thrush. Pigeons bounced in the shiny air above the trees, climbing steeply then sinking down with a double wing-clap of exultation, and there was an ecstasy of freedom and celebration in the swoop that transmitted itself to my breast, so that I too seemed borne into the air and swung forward on wings. A jay was hopping heavily about the ground — and it struck me that I could not remember seeing a jay hopping before — and, as I came level with a gap in the trees, I saw a solitary magpie feeding with a rook flock in a field where daisies shone like pearl buttons. In a glade where bluebell shoots were thick and white I found a dead cock pheasant jammed by its neck in the first fork of a young ash. Around the ankle of the tree was a circle of scratches and claw-marks, probably the marks left by frustrated rats which had tried to reach the corpse.

The land climbed and the wood thinned. Now there was a plantation, recently drastically cut, and primroses glowed in massed bouquets, great extravagant splurges of rich colour. I knew, although I had not been this far before, that I was ascending the great whale-back ridge of hills that stretched for six miles along the Gedd Valley, ending in a blunt snout above the market town where we had our Saturday stall. I had not brought the map with me but I estimated that I was going to top the ridge at Mule Dell, a spot I had pinpointed for eventual attention during my winter evening poring over the Ordnance Survey two-and-a-half miles to one mile map. I sweated on, and found that I was beginning to give less attention to my surroundings and more to the grinding aching soreness in my groin. Yet even that could not make me turn back now. I had struck an excellent bargain with this April day and I wanted my money's worth.

Trees stopped growing so casually. Up here it was necessary to work hard for a living. Even the hedges that went up the bland expansive land like dusky snakes were skinnier, a bit more muscular, a bit less flabbily corpulent than those on the lower level. They held many magpies' nests, most of them tattered and crumbled but there was one in a whitened blackthorn that was new and nearly ready, and I heard the anxious clucking of a bird somewhere out of sight.

As I drove near the top of the ridge I found myself thinking of stone-curlews, for, in this bare, clean, long-limbed country there should have been stone-curlews. But, of course, there were not, for, like so many other birds and animals, this is a species which has retreated to a few last-stand centres where circumstances make it comparatively secure from man and his myriad nuisances. What were there was a kestrel, spearing the sky with his incredibly delicately designed wings and showing me the lovely russet of his back, and a hare lolloping a mile below. I turned into the wind that scoured the earth and began the long walk along the crest to the distant Pedler's Hill.

The kestrel was hovering away to my left, a curved question mark in the sky, and beyond I could see sheep grazing in the valley bottom, small and fluffy white as dandelion clocks. The wind became troublesome. Up here it was really cold. The gusts struck my body like hailstones through the shimmering sunlight. I decided to abandon the crest, and branched at a shallow angle down the hillside where lapwings were tumbling and wailing above the frail copse. Rooks; more magpies; three more hares, one sitting in an upright outraged stance and looking like an offended baby kangaroo; ten journeying house martins, the first, flying hard above the roof of a scraggy wood. Then, as my head was turned to watch a carrion crow skulking away from a hedgerow elm a mile below, I stumbled to my knees.

On all fours in the heap of earth that had tripped me I stared down into the darkness of a wide, deep hole. It was not the only hole. Here in the stony flank of this naked hillside were four more, set in a line at intervals of about ten feet, and before each was a cascade of creamy soil.

Now quite clearly they were the work of badgers. I had been told that there were badgers in the district, and the size of the holes, the drifts of soft excavated earth, the litter of discarded bedding, left no cause for doubt. Yet this was altogether an odd affair for according to the textbook rules badgers should not have tunnelled in such a brazenly exposed position as this; they ought to have rooted around for deep cover and seclusion, and bored their holes in a matted thorn brake or a woodland dell. And here was this sett, a good mile from trees – and those no more than an emaciated, wind-pummelled copse.

It pricked my curiosity. I got up and dusted my trousers. I peered down those yawning holes but there was nothing but the silence of utter darkness, and I wondered if, within the solid chest of the hill, there was a family of badgers curled up asleep like streaky-faced bears. I turned my attention to the earth piles before the holes and thoughtfully kicked at them. There were tangles of dry dead grass and wintered fern fronds, and then my toecap hit something heavier yet which was lighter than a stone. I picked it up and when I had knocked off the crust of earth I saw that the knotted lump was a ligament of old root. Of course! I rummaged in the earth and found many more fragments.

The root-chips slotted like pre-designed clues into a detective story, and the plot became clear and logical. Once trees had grown here – perhaps a century, perhaps a decade before – and deep amid them the badgers had had their sett. Later the wood had been cleared to give grazing for sheep and the secret tunnels were exposed to daylight. Turning, I gazed down the scooping land and saw that wavering away from the holes were many thin, hard-beaten tracks which struck the distant hedges and reappeared, ribbon-like, across the farther meadow: the trails worn by the pads of generations of badgers. The last lingering doubt as to whether the sett was still occupied vanished. Gazing at those well-trodden paths, I knew now for sure that the badgers had not gone. Certainly, they were there now, curled up asleep beneath my feet in the blackness of their grass-cushioned caves; and when the spring moon rose they would come shuffling out to take the paths of their forefathers to the rabbit-rich hunting country of the valley.

As I stood in the bright, cold April light it gave me an odd satisfaction to think of those invisible slumbering badgers. They had known their world torn up by its roots. They had listened to the thud of footsteps and the clank of axes overhead. They had dug themselves out of their mutilated tunnels and seen the awful change about them. Yet they had stayed on among the ruins and with an obstinate contempt for the interference of stronger forces, they had clung to their ancient home, made their adjustments and carried on. The ruins had gone now; the invading forces had retreated. It was still the badgers' hill.

Chapter Fourteen

Community-owned livestock was not numerous. There were a few dogs and cats belonging to various people, but pet animals were not encouraged. There had been far too many quarrels and resentments in the past caused by messes within the house, for no pet-owner would believe it possible that his own animal was guilty, and, therefore, refused to accept responsibility for the clearing up. So, although there was no ban, supervision was applied so rigorously (about the only rule that Bereworde ever firmly kept to) by non-pet-owners that most families preferred to stay petless. We, of course, had Bambi, and later her pups. Mrs Baxter had a she-Scottie which was perpetually at her side on the end of a tartan lead. Indeed the Scottie was, for a short period, the centre of some interested speculation, for she appeared to have figured in a canine immaculate conception. Never, as far as could be judged, more than a foot from Mrs Baxter's skirt hem, she one day, to the consternation of the old lady who had remained unsuspecting until that moment, produced a litter of coarse-haired ginger puppies: which Mrs Baxter immediately drowned. There were also two guinea pigs belonging to the Harper children, one of which was – to our surprise – munched up by Bambi. There was also a communally-owned goat, which, in one day, ate the best part of a seat of a sofa stored temporarily in the stables. There was also the poultry.

Looking after the poultry was a rota-job, although Hilary Harper did most of the work. But, sooner or later, everyone took a turn in the feeding, the egg-collecting and the pen-cleaning. There were some who did not much care for the job because of the menace of the gander, a heavy, brutish, vicious-tempered bird whose beak had dug most calves. The gander had two geese which he ruled tyrannically. One bore the name of Susan, and it was Susan who that spring figured in an incident of even more intriguing mystery than the pregnancy of Mrs Baxter's Scottie.

The curious affair started on a day in May when I carelessly sent a broken plastic plate rolling into the orbit of Susan's life. It had been Amanda's plate until she snapped a large triangle out of the edge by rapping it on her high chair in aggressive demand for more bacon. After that it joined the children's arsenal of peculiar instruments in the derelict barn, its dedicated purpose being for the making of mud pies. Not long after, I saw it on the lower lawn, a stained, chipped caricature of the shining scarlet kitchenware that it had been a few weeks earlier. Irresponsibly I kicked it and it arced away to land rolling in the squalid plot where the geese and chickens live. Its discarding was final. Yet, unexpectedly, like the rehabilitation of a tramp, there opened in its unindividualistic die-stamped life a new significant phase.

It was a week later that Bee remarked as she came indoors with a colander of eggs, 'I think Susan has pulled it off at last. She's sitting very determinedly in the nettles.'

That was excellent news. Up to then Susan had produced not a single egg in return for her keep. I went to look and found her crouched and low and widespread in a dell in the nettles. Not wishing to disrupt her new-found sense of duty, I stood looking down on her benignly from a distance. She eyed me with beady suspicion but remained squatted motionless upon her nest.

A dunnock flipped up to a bare bough above her head and trilled. I noticed that the wild apple at the edge of the wood was frothing like the most glamourized shaving cream advertisement. Pleased with Susan's show of social consciousness, I walked on through the chicken run without feeling even a twinge of resentment towards the two fleeing jackdaws which, as usual, had been busy stealing the chickens' food. A cock chaffinch, looking as if arrayed for a carnival, was singing ardently from the fence, and a young rabbit, smaller than Amanda's smallest woolly toy, galloped unsteadily into the wood. The sun shone and everything seemed very right and proper and in its correct place.

On my way back I noticed that Susan had left her nest to get her share of dinner. Stepping over to the nettles I saw that deep in the cushion of grey down were two rather dingy eggs. She came waddling back to them, and I slipped away.

Two mornings later the queer business started. It was Andrew who ran into the house shouting excitedly, 'Daddy, Susan has thrown away her eggs!' Indeed she had. To my dismay the eggs were scattered heedlessly among the nettles – but Susan was still crouched purposefully on her nest. Thinking that it was altogether odd, I shoved her off. In the centre of the nest was the broken plastic plate.

It was quite a shock. It was something like having that Shaggy Dog story spring to life – the one about walking into your bathroom and finding a horse sitting in the bath. There was no apparent logical reason for it being there.

I dealt with the situation decisively. The plate was sent skidding away and the eggs replaced in their rightful place. I left Susan hunched stupidly beside the nest, repenting of her foolishness, I hoped, and walked back to the house wondering if any of the children had been playing a joke. After a few questions it was plain they knew nothing about it.

An hour later I made another inspection. The eggs had again been ejected. This time I was none too gentle as I pushed Susan off the nest, knowing what I would find. Yes, there was the unpleasant plate, glowing with warmth from Susan's embrace. Angry thoughts darted through my head, thoughts of fragmenting the plate with my heel, thoughts of despatching Susan to another much larger plate via the oven. Yet she looked so unhappy, in a dull confused sort of way, that I stayed my hand. Presumably she would grow out of her idiotic attachment.

Eventually she did. But for a week, while her eggs addled with neglect, she was inseparable from the plate. Hour after hour, through the hot, still days, she brooded it, seeming unconcerned that her devotion brought about no change to its battered inanimate flatness. Many times I was tempted to end the nonsense, but I was prevented by a vague fear of doing Susan some irreparable psychological harm, so that for the rest of her days she would be a neurotic, barred from a happy normal life by a fixation for plates.

Then one day I was relieved to see that she was with the other goose at the bottom of the orchard. I found the plate, cold and deserted in a clump of dock. With a quick surreptitious movement I picked it up. I went straight to the coal yard and there I smashed it to little bits with a hammer. The bits were placed deep within the dustbin.

That, we all hoped, was the end of Freudian complications in the simple and straightforward routine of the garden. But I was not absolutely sure that my action was not in itself a piece of symbolic revenge.

While all this was going on a new Berewordean had arrived. His enrolment was not pre-arranged. He came back with me one afternoon, carried in a sheep-skin driving gauntlet. Then, because he was less than a month old, he showed few signs of the patent-leather smartness that he was going to display as an adult magpie. He was lousy, tatter-feathered and dolorous-mouthed. For all that, he was probably the most universally popular member the community ever had. This is how he came, and sadly went.

A friend who was spending the weekend with me had brought with him a wallet bulging with rings, the British Museum bird rings. How many nests had I ready for ringing? he wanted to know. Well, I said, a fortnight ago I had seen a pair of chiffchaffs carrying nesting material into the nettles beside the old air-raid shelter in the ha-ha ditch. And I thought the pied wagtails were nesting this year in the drainpipe beside the door arch. Little owls, I was pretty sure, had settled in the Turkey oak at the bottom of the Park Field. I *did* know for sure that a blackbird was sitting on a nest balanced on the creeper on the stable wall, but I wasn't sure which hole the nuthatches had picked in the walnut.

It sounded a vague and bitty list, and Paul's grunt increased my feeling of guilt at my unscientific methods. Instead of lazing about the lower lawn, or poking haphazardly into a hedge, or watching the rooks through my binoculars, I should have been organizing the spring by making an orderly and documented survey of the estate. I knew I couldn't even have begun to compose a treatise for *British Birds* on the territory of robins around the house.

My friend belonged to the New Naturalist school: he was keen, intent, businesslike; his pencil was perpetually rippling across his notebook; he made me feel old-fashioned, a foolish dilettante. I followed him out through the stable yard and we started work at the top of the orchard.

It was an enjoyable day. It seemed years since I had bird-nested with such thoroughness. First we found a goldfinch's nest, half built, in the mast-rigging of a heavy old yew close to the lodge. The two graceful little birds, with their mardi-gras masks of red and white and black, were flitting back and forth with cargoes of lichen and spider-silk, which they were building delicately into a substantial cup. I had been right about the chiffchaffs. Some self-confidence returned when we found the globe of wizened leaves down among the nettle trunks, and the hen slipped like a blown lime leaf off the half dozen minute eggs as we peered in. The wagtails, too, helped to save my reputation, for there was a nest with eggs blocking the iron head of the drainpipe.

None of these could be worked on but within an hour we had found four thrushes' nests with young, and these were ringed. Each nestling was taken out in turn, and, while it was firmly but gently caged in one hand, a ring was pressed round a leg. Then it was put back beside its brothers and sisters.

All the time we were quartering the shrubberies the rooks were up, hoarsely yelling and making a spinning wheel of shadow on the grass, with its embroidery of bugle sprigs and the bright new sovereigns of celandines. Most of the rooks' nests were built in the big beeches that grouped around the entrance to the ride, but every pine had one or more dark rosettes in its bobbed head. There were young ones in most of the nests. Their scrawny necks jerked about above the lips.

My friend decided to take his rings up to the rooks. The beeches were impossible but the pines, once the first fifteen feet had been monkey-climbed, were natural ladders. He started off on the most convenient-looking.

While his feet were scrabbling for the first hold, every adult rook in the colony was up, screaming outrage. Once at the first branch, he climbed rapidly. But it was a wasted mission, for as he drew nearer the three nests in the crown I could see the fledgling rooks getting jumpier and jumpier in their fear, and when he was more than ten feet from the lowest nest, they began, in ones and twos, to flop overboard and tumble to earth like shot-up parachutes. Paul had nothing but three empty nests on his hands; down below the young rooks flapped and hopped into hiding. Plainly, the time for ringing rooks had passed for this season.

He descended the pine and I got the car out of the stable. We drove down Pedler's Hill to the valley. I turned it into a cart track and we left it beside a haystack. On foot we began to climb back across the fields up the hill line. On the way I showed him the badgers' sett. Since I had last seen it there had been another house-cleaning. There were fresh scatterings of used bedding outside the holes. We went on, topped the ridge and made for the long, broad stretch of Breach Wood that swam with a vivid new greenness in the sun. It was May and the voices of warblers were in the wind. Where bluebells washed the trees with sky tints a blackcap was singing and there were willow warblers and chiffchaffs filling the air with gay sound. We found three young tawny owls in a snapped-off oak and ringed them, and in an attempt to trace the turtle dove that was groaning somewhere in a place of dense green, we came upon another badgers' sett — this, unlike the unorthodox hillside one, typical of its kind, dug in the steep side of a glade. There were four holes, and, again, well-marked paths threaded away in all directions. One led to the edge of a wood, through a gap in the fence, and across the cowslip-daubed meadow to a pond.

A nightingale was pealing in the brushy edge, its voice half-drowned by the bellow of a cuckoo, as we walked back towards the lane. It was half way down the field that we came upon the magpie's nest. We noticed one of the adult birds dodging away when we were half a mile above and found the nest without difficulty. It was while Paul was ringing the five young ones that the idea seized me.

'Bring one of them down with you,' I called up to him. He did, and with it tucked in a fold of my jacket, I carried it back to the car. I pushed it into the warm fold of the driving gauntlet, placed it on the back seat, and we drove back to Bereworde.

At first I kept it in the children's room, in an old, bent canary cage fished out of the dusk of the stable loft. But after only a few days it was no longer necessary to keep it caged. Confidence flowed into it in tidal waves. At the opening of the door it set up a strident chirruping for food, and, as its wings gained strength and sense of purpose, it began flying freely about our floor.

It became the community's court jester. Wherever there were people the magpie was certain to be, for it loved crowds as much as a Margate August Bank Holidayer. Its impudence was limitless, its curiosity no less. It lived a gipsy life within the estate, because, unpinioned and uncaged, it went where it wanted to go and sponged on whoever was handy. When it first left the canary cage I erected within the log rotunda a sleeping shelter equipped with food table, out of reach of cats. My theory was that this would encourage it to use the rotunda as its headquarters. But the magpie, upon being carried there and placed meaningfully upon the table, flicked its splendid tail contemptuously and flapped away to more interesting places. In any case there was no cause for misgivings about cats. The magpie took care of himself (or herself, for it was never satisfactorily sexed) very adequately. In the beginning the burly rusty-black tom belonging to Ruthene took a gruesomely ominous interest in this flamboyant bird that was loitering about the place with such tempting clumsiness. But although as far as I know no human was in the neighbourhood at the time, I am quite certain that the magpie gave the cat clearly to understand that he was not to be persecuted. I judged this from the way cat or dog always slunk hastily away with surly backward glances when the magpie flaunted on to the scene, and I guessed that one or two lethal jabs from that long spear of a beak had changed the balance of power. Certainly the magpie was not afraid of them, no more afraid of them than she was of the goat, which she invariably attacked with a boisterous cackle and sent bleating into shelter.

The magpie's indelicate behaviour caused me some worry, because I suspected that before long it was going to be one of those squibs that exploded at family meetings, suddenly revealing that there was a lot of compressed irritation concentrated upon something one had oneself not particularly noticed. Yet that never happened and on the whole the community seemed to find it amusing to have a magpie suddenly alighting on a bedroom windowsill or hopping swaggeringly inside to see what food there was to be stolen or bright trinket to be played with. Certainly the children adored it, and although Baby Amanda and the younger set were a little rougher with their eager embraces than the magpie cared for, it seemed to enjoy being the middle of a sand-pit rough-house and to find riding around on the proud shoulder of Andrew or Timmy an easy way of getting effortless transport. As the children soon discovered, it loved to have its pate scratched, and squatted with fluttering lids and an expression of sensual pleasure for as long as one wished to continue.

During the first part of the summer the magpie added a great deal of amusement and colour to community life. And then, abruptly as he came, he was gone.

One evening I was hurrying across the terrace into the stable yard with a letter in my hand. The newspaper article that should have been in the afternoon post for London had been put off and put off. Now, with it mercifully trapped inside the sealed envelope, I had to get the car out of the stable – past the barrier of broken prams and empty oil drums, always re-erected by the children – and drive the eight miles to town to catch the post. There was no collection from the village box after midday.

I stopped suddenly. In the round yellow rubber dinghy, once carried in the belly of a Short Stirling of Bomber Command, was floating something small and black with a dab of white on its limp shape. Putting the envelope in my pocket, I went down the steps and fished it out. It was the magpie, and as I held the body by the half-grown shot-green tail, muddy water dribbled from its parted beak.

The dinghy was the children's paddle pool. For a month or so of powerful heat, of days varnished blue and yellow by the sky's prismal light, the dinghy had been the focal point of a swarm of corn-brown young bodies; a lovely sight. There was another pool, down at the edge of the orchard, hidden by the rockery and primpy suburban garden shrubs planted by some Victorian owner. It was too far away for safety and was empty but for a foot-deep puddle at one end, a pool of black, stinking water, vibrant with microbe life, where the frogs had their clammy orgies. (One male had for three days been holding in fervent necrophilic embrace the drifting fungus-yellow corpse of a thrice-larger female.) The magpie loved to be with the children and perhaps because they were always about the dinghy had flap-hopped along to find them in the cool of the previous evening when they were all in bed and the garden was quiet with shadow, I thought as I stood holding his soaked body. Perhaps, finding no-one there, he had vaulted up on to the rim. Always curious of movement or colour or sound, perhaps he had espied his reflection in the mud-oranged water, craned forward to see more closely, and slithered in. And because he was young and still not maturely strong, his wings had been unable to save him from drowning.

I pushed through the bushes and took the magpie to the compost heap. There I laid him on the grass-cuttings. He had given joy to children in his life, now he would give richness to the soil.

Next day the news had to be broken to the children. There were dejected faces for a while and a funeral procession was made to the dinghy to see where the magpie had ended his short, merry life. But when I passed half an hour later, the screaming and splashing and the flash of nude bodies did not seem subdued by sorrow: it was an incident, sad but irremediable; there, in the child's logical and dispassionate assessment, the matter ended.

Chapter Fifteen

The end? How did the end come? Perhaps it started – for us – that September day that we moved in. For sure, the factors that ultimately sanded the community's carburettor were then already filtering in. The reasons for the disintegration cannot be stated in complete detail. Certainly the money problem, which billowed into ever larger proportions until, like an atom bomb mushroom, it hung in a pall over our life at Bereworde, was a powerful factor. But there were other fundamental causes which perhaps it would be simplest to label ideological. Probably sharpened by the financial worry, personal conflicts grew more pronounced. Most of the time they remained submerged beneath a makeshift day-to-day agreement to disagree, but now and then they exploded with a suddenness and force that revealed with discomforting clarity a bitterness that had not been apparent when we first moved in. I remember an incident that occurred in that fluid period when the future of the community seemed to be dissolving in grey confusion. There had been some dissatisfaction with the housekeeping and the meals we were getting, and a few people, including me, felt it was a subject that should be dealt with at a family meeting. Anna and I were talking about it as we returned from feeding the chickens. Beside the rotunda we met Aubrey, dressed for logging in his Army sock-cap and Service boots.

'Look, Aubrey,' I said, 'Anna and I have been talking about this food business and we think it ought to be put on a better organized basis. Will you put it on the agenda for tonight's meeting?'

'No, I don't think it would be proper to do that. The new housekeeper has been doing the job only a month. It is a time of exceptional difficulty now that we have no cook. I do not think it would be right to question her authority in that way.'

'Well, Aubrey, I don't agree,' Anna remarked. 'Naturally we all know the difficulties. After all, all the women are having to do the cooking. For that reason I think we ought to have more say in how the materials for cooking are provided and what they are. Anyway, it's not a question of *authority*.'

'Besides,' I put in, 'you can't refuse to put something on the agenda if a member of the community wants it on.'

He ignored me and turned his round spectacled eyes solemnly upon Anna. 'I repeat that I do not consider we should line ourselves up against her in the way you are suggesting.'

Wearily, Anna said, 'I'm not suggesting anything of the sort, Aubrey. I'm not lining myself up against anyone, I'm merely asking for this matter to be openly discussed. In any case why should the position of housekeeper suddenly have become sacrosanct?'

'We must give her absolute loyalty.'

'Bunkum,' I said. 'I don't give absolute loyalty to anything if I consider it doesn't deserve it. What a curious principle to introduce, Aubrey.'

His Catholic conscience flared to furnace heat. His eyes glittered and he began to go tight at the mouth as he did in the mornings when the car was honking impatiently. 'No, Ken, perhaps that's the trouble with Bereworde, no-one knows the meaning of loyalty.'

It was an absurd and meaningless quarrel, because actually there was no substance to it. The difference of opinion about the housekeeping was really quite irrelevant. What had occurred was an impact between two different attitudes to the community in general, and this trivial matter had accidentally provided the electric contact.

There was a similarly bad-tempered scene during the next family meeting but one, when the subject of Ruthene's wandering cat was raised. The cat had been the cause of some annoyance. Its favourite sleeping site was an occupied cot. Several times Bee had thrown it out of Amanda's cot, and it had been found curled up on most of the other children's beds. It was a fat, weighty animal and would have had no difficulty in suffocating a baby had it decided to sleep on its face. Ruthene had been warned several times to keep the cat under stricter control, but the nuisance went on. On his way to the family meeting

John Harper found the cat on Miff's bed. His normal truculence mounted to storm proportions and during Any Other Business he put forward a resolution that Ruthene be instructed to get rid of her cat forthwith.

I supported this for Amanda's sake, but I was startled by the vehemence with which the arguments were put. Again, quite clearly, it was not such a trifling matter as it might appear in the minute book. It was another outbreak of war between two sides which were rapidly taking on recognizable entities. Voices were raised and a few unconnected but often accurate criticisms made of the behaviour and attitude of certain Berewordeans. The incident ended with Ruthene, her blasé airiness destroyed by the attack upon her cat, rushing from the room in tears, and the meeting proceeded in an ugly calm towards its end.

One became more and more aware of a spirit of intrigue sneaking into daily life. One met two or three people talking on the stairs, and the talk stilled for a few seconds until one had passed. One saw social visits being conducted between unexpected allies. And rumour began to circulate at a dynamic rate.

The first family to acknowledge publicly the so far unadmitted split were the Sullivans. At last Ham decided definitely to go, and he went after having loudly reversed all his original enthusiastic praises of the Bereworde manner of living. During this time Mary Stubbs had been in hospital, and suddenly she died. Jim, who had been staying in London to be near her, returned and told us that for obvious reasons he felt he no longer wanted to stay on, and, with everyone's sympathetic understanding, he got together his belongings and departed, leaving the community very much weaker and a less happy place by his going. Then it was Aubrey's turn. He and Gladys, he declared in a pulpit boom at one Sunday supper time, had come to the conclusion that they must, reluctantly, leave Bereworde. It was a decision taken with the greatest regret, but recent events in connection with their children had made that decision inevitable. Also the old spirit seemed to have disappeared. He did not think it was necessary to say more than that.

It was not necessary. Everyone knew what was troubling Aubrey. Again, it was a thing which went right down to the foundations of the community and the gap in outlook between the Morrises, with their tentative Catholic 'radicalness', and what I call the Reichians was too profound and too wide to be spanned at this stage by philosophical argument or efforts to reconstitute the community. The snag upon which Aubrey had chosen to hang his resignation speech was the one of child upbringing. When we had first gone to Bereworde I had noticed, even then, a divergence of opinion within the generally enlightened atmosphere. As I said, no child, as far as I know, was ever beaten at Bereworde and at best they were allowed the space of a prairie for self-expression. But the space varied in degrees from parent to parent. Although, in those happier times of a year before, everyone there would staunchly have declared that they stood in opposition to discipline, discipline was in fact applied. I call it unjustified and undefendable discipline when a child of six is denied fairy stories and adventure books, and given Shakespeare and Donne to read. I call it bad discipline constantly to nag a child about its lack of success at school. I call it equally bad discipline to allow a child to wreck everything its hands encounter, although in this case the fault is of a different brand, for in that sort of immature violence is an attempt at retaliation. All these things happened at Bereworde at the instance of different parents. But they were not the reasons for the Morrises' departure. That was, superficially, the contact of their children with pagan children, whose language and behaviour did not always accord with those laid down by the Church.

This little clutch of resignations forced the situation out into the open. At a specially convened family meeting held in the Harpers' room John showed that if Bereworde were wound up at that moment there would be a deficit of about nine hundred pounds. There were voices raised against the proposal implicit in this statement. Julian, whose migratory visits to Bereworde perhaps denied him full appreci-ation of the magnitude of the problems, urged that every effort should be made to keep the community going.

'Let's have a bing-bang advertising campaign and get in another set of families as replacements,' he said. 'With the right approach we should get enough applications to allow us to pick the right people. In the mean time, there'll have to be even more stringent economizing.'

This was received in silence. What did we all want? What did I want? Did I want Bereworde to go on, in the restless, uncertain, bickering atmosphere of recent weeks, in the hope that there would suddenly be a resurgence of the spirit of which Aubrey had spoken –

and which perhaps, as in the case of so many ideals, was the glister that rubs off with the newness? Within myself I suspected that I did not want a negative drift onwards, that I would welcome a hard, clear-cut decision, no matter how calamitous it might be.

Midnight came and went and discussion plodded on through the cigarette smoke, and when the momentum was slowing through exhaustion a vote was taken. By a majority of three it was decided that the community should be closed. The voting alignment was interesting, and, in a way, funny. Those who supported the proposal that the community should continue were the very people who all along had shown least enthusiasm for communal activity, who, in fact, had fairly well succeeded in transforming Bereworde from a community into a block of self-contained flats. The debate that I had conducted in my own mind (and I knew that Bee's reasoning had run on closely similar lines) resulted in me voting for the dissolution. I did so not because I wanted the community to end, but because I knew that if it continued in name it would not for very much longer be a community worth living in. I felt, in a mixed emotional way, that by pronouncing death sentence upon it now, at least a few of the embodied ideals could be preserved. Anna, of us all the most devoutly dedicated to the original aims, also voted against going on, and she explained her stand by saying, 'At last I feel I can speak completely frankly about the situation. For too long I've felt frustrated in practically everything I've tried to do in the community. I'm tired of trying to live in two camps at once. I don't any longer want to have to eat white bread because I'm in the minority wanting to eat wholemeal, and being told it therefore isn't worth getting it. I feel my life has been governed too monopolistically by ideas that I don't share, and I'm not prepared to go on in this way any longer.'

After that the details of the closing down were tackled. There was lengthy talk on how any profits on sale should be divided and also how responsibility for debts should be allocated among past and present Berewordeans. The debts were roughly divided into two categories: those to outside creditors, and those listed under loans advanced by members of the community. It was agreed that a debts committee should be set up.

Three days later another meeting was hastily called, for now that the decision had been taken there was much to attend to. A variety of economies were worked out and it was settled that from now on there should be a minimum of expenditure on the house, on only essential repairs advantageous to the sale. The final matter was the actual date of closing. The Barlows had given notice and it seemed obvious that it would be pointless to keep the house open with only a few families in residence. An outline plan for a mass move out to the cottages and lodge was put on paper.

The repercussion upon Bee and me was one of profound gloom and anxiety. In simple terms it meant that in a few months at the most we would have nowhere to live; that we had to find somewhere else, and a comparison between my bank account and the prices of houses (or flats, which were invariably available only upon payment of a legalized bribe called a premium) did not make it easy to see what we could do about it. However another hope arose. The following weekend Anna came up to our room and explained that she and Ian were still determined to continue community life. There was to be a fresh start, this time on the right lines, and this time sticking to them. Would we feel like joining in another and smaller group together with the Harpers and the Camerons? The four families had a similarity of ideas that the others did not have, she felt. Despite the drawbacks that I had found at Berewordxe, Bee and I, after a private talk, decided we would join in. We told Anna and she asked us to come to a meeting of the four families that evening and to bring with us a statement of the foundations upon which we would like to see the new community established.

We took along an affidavit, which read:

Children. We think it would be pleasant to see a little more responsibility for each others' children, i.e. not ignoring a crying or miserable child, if, this time, it is not one's own. Also to apply Reichian principles to other people's children, i.e. when a child is doing something of which we disapprove but which, if done by one's own child, would perhaps be tackled differently. *The House*. While the price factor, distance from work, etc., all impose limitations upon the setting of the new community, we feel that it is important that it should be in real country and not in a Hampstead Garden Suburb fake-up. This hinges on the last paragraph, for apart from our personal preferences, we want our children to grow up in intimate relationship and with intimate knowledge and understanding of the natural world. The roots of the sound life are in the country. Also, we think it important that the house should be good to look at, for it will be the background against which the community will be developing and against which our children will be growing up. *Food*. We are ready, even eager, to try a thorough-going food reform diet, and hope that this will provide not only more healthy, more sensibly balanced meals, but also meals of better quality than heretofore. We think, too, that the Bereworde Sunday family tea tradition might be extended on a community basis to having the children into one or two more meals during the weekend in the adults' dining-room with their parents, each family perhaps having their own table. This would combine for the children the fun of family tea with the enjoyment of having it with the other children. It would also to an extent overcome their feeling of exclusion from the adults' dining-room. We also favour as an experiment the proposal for cooked midday dinner with high tea in the evening – the hope being that it would cut down the time spent eating and thereby lengthen the evening. We would also like to see community responsibility and morality honoured by the abolition of private rations and the introduction of the normal family practice of fruit-on-the-sideboard and biscuits-in-the-cupboard (finances allowing). *The Women*. Our hope is that a new spirit and a new composition will give the womenfolk a less harrassing, arduous and nerve-fraying existence than at present. They should be able to take their children (or someone else's children) out for a casual afternoon stroll if they feel like it, without a nagging guilt. In fact, the whole tempo of their domestic life needs slowing, and I see no reason why this should not be quite practical in a community where responsibilities are shared in a responsible manner. *House Duties*. Bee hopes that all cooking will be shared by the women, but that help is enrolled for basic domestic chores. She also strongly recommends the abolition of the rota system. This should not be difficult; for example servers at meals will not be needed as before, and broadly, the work should be done voluntarily more easily and in a happier frame of mind than has been the case amid the conflicting temperaments of the present set-up. *Rules*. We propose one new rule – No Rules. Among adult, mature people (which we are not but hope to become) schoolroom discipline should not be necessary. The way to settle divisions of opinion is by mutual agreement. It hardly needs stating that if our children are being reared on Reichian lines, rules are an anachronism. *Relationships*. An attitude Bee would like to see left behind in Bereworde is the 'holier than thou' approach to the omissions and failings of others. Can it be hoped that one's own personal responsibilities will be fulfilled before outraged attention is given to the unfulfilled responsibilities of other people? It should be possible sometimes to clean up someone else's mess without feeling martyred. *Finance*. We favour the idea of renting if it is possible as this would be a fairer apportioning of the burden that the new house will inevitably be. As for future costs-per-family, we feel that we could – just – manage to pay the present rate, but would like to see ancillary expenses included, i.e. coffee, fruit, etc. *Summing Up*. The most important factor of all, we feel, will be the spirit in which the new community is founded and fostered. Love, understanding, flexibility and a positive belief in the experiment are the things needed.

But the hopes and affidavits evaporated like steam. During the next few weeks we did a great deal of house-hunting in a variety of cars. We saw farmhouses and small manors, company directors' country seats and knocked-together cottages, and there seemed to be one or two which might be suitable for the four families' needs if they were still in the market when a buyer had been found for Bereworde. It was wasted effort. The reconstituted community never came into existence. During the upheaval, John's and Gerald's photography business, which had been floundering into rougher water, hit a financial rock. The strain felled John and he moved into bed with a bad outbreak of his old ulcer. It was while there that he made up his mind completely to cut free. He informed Gerald that he was withdrawing from the partnership and going on the land. Not many weeks later he and Hilary moved out and, after a short agricultural course under the Government training scheme, he began a new life as a farm labourer on an organic farm in Dorset. The Camerons also changed their minds. Alec had not been well, either. For him, the chief obstacle to Bereworde had always been its distance from his office. He came to the conclusion that he no longer wanted to live in the country, and finally they acquired a house in a London suburb.

Our departure was not so easily settled. Somehow, somewhere, we had to find a place to rent, for buying seemed to be out of the question. During those next months most of our time was spent in writing to estate agents, replying to advertisements and going on long futile drives in the Home Counties to visit impossible houses.

When it had been agreed that Bereworde should be sold it appeared that it would all be over in a few weeks. In fact the end ran a protracted course. After a little time the feeling of disaster faded and life went on with comparative calm. Outside the house, which now had many echoing empty spaces, the grounds were mellowly lovely with summer. Swallows were feeding their young in the stables and the flycatchers, which had their nest on the ledge above the Parfitts' bathroom window, performed their lively aerial dances in chase of insects above the terrace. Through the hot, suspended days a turtle dove droned. I had found its nest – built less than 4 feet high in the ruined pergola – which seemed to have been placed with an aesthetic appreciation of surroundings, for the two pinkish-white eggs were framed by splashes of gorgeous bloom-dusty pink roses. For a time, when the crisis had been at its peak, I had been unable to write because of the worry that dragged at my mind. But when summer was becoming a little raddled with rust-edged leaves and withered flowers, I was again regularly shutting myself in the tiny cell-like room to complete the painfully long-drawn labour on the tale of the boy outlaws.

One day, at a difficult passage, I got up from the table and stepped over to the window. There it all was, and I wondered for how much longer I would be looking at it: the placed stretch of countryside to the far-away buxomness of Ashcroft Park where Queen Elizabeth had spent part of her childhood. A worm of irritation stirred within me. Suddenly there seemed to be a stagnation about the scene that depressed me. It was so still, so changelessly ordinary, so lifeless. Did nothing ever happen out there except the gradual, subtle, seasonal change of colour and tone – over-subtle, too gradual? Or perhaps it did. Perhaps the worry of the past few weeks and the awful domination of my mind by this book had killed my senses. All right, I would check on that.

I went back to the table and got a sheet of paper and I lifted my binoculars down from the wall-peg. For the next hour – I glanced at my watch — I would keep a timetable. This would settle it one way or the other. I drew up a chair and settled down. When the hour had passed this was the record I had on the paper.

Day warm, still, grey, rain-menacing. 12.45 pm. Park Field blank, a yawn of green. A flock of rooks billow up from the little oblong field that is invisible from here in the tuck of the tall, ragged hedgerow. They charge across the brow of the hill like a brigade of black cavalry, slow, gyrate and break formation, then haphazardly come in to land. They string out across the Park Field and begin feeding busily, swaggering about, upright with a bit of a roll in their gait, and cracking their pricker-like beaks down to the ground. There are 43 rooks; no jackdaws.

12.47. Four wood-pigeons and one stock-dove fly over, prospectively, half-circle the field then go on towards the village. One of the pigeons performs that lovely heart-soaring flight-spring and swoop that never fails to give me a scenic-railway sensation.

12.48. Over the brow strut three wood-pigeons, portly and town-councillory. They feed separate from the rooks and they are quicker in their movements. Their gulp-rate must be considerably higher; they have the greedy momentum of men who have been too successful and who live too well.

12.50. There is an oak that grows by the lower fence, and some of its upper limbs have withered and become barren. The branches are twisty as Sir Harry Lauder's walking stick and jut high and clear of the crimped thick leaves below. These branches are a stopping place in constant use by birds flying north, south, east and west across the grounds. A perch up there gives a bird an uninterrupted view all round. A month ago there seemed never to be a cuckoo missing from the highest stub. At this moment it is occupied by a spotted flycatcher. There are two flycatchers there (no doubt the pair with young on the window moulding nest below me) and they are loitering lazily in the oak, jerking into little spasms of fly-chasing flight, then back to their perch. A sound that is like a squeaking wheelbarrow is coming from their beaks.

12.54. The sun has burst through, shouldering its way out of the clouds and radiating a phoney self-confidence. Another 13 rooks came into the Park Field and in the sunshine they shimmer oilily, looking as though gowned in that material worn by night club singers in Hollywood films. Some jackdaws follow them. I thought they would be along soon. They follow the rooks about like small boys tagging on to a gang of older, admired boys. Some of them are this year's young, browner and without much grey cowling. They may even be the ones that grew up in the chimney above this room and irritated me during June with their incessant yapping.

12.57. A rook makes a three-point landing. Simultaneously the ground was hit by out-poked legs and beak which began digging instantly. A pied wagtail has just landed on the gravel path and is doing a delicate ballet as it pinches up midges; then it ripples away over the house to its young in the drainpipe.

1.30. Under the sun's white stare the fields over to the south-west look like a sterile yellowish-white. Sheaves are laying about in some, but two are bristly-bare, empty, temporarily used-up. There is a glare of colour in the meadow nearer at hand, a jumble-sale stall of piled poppies, hawkbits and scabious. Even nearer, along the hedge marked by a wayfaring tree with berry-clusters of three different colours, red, red-white and red-purple, are splotches of woody nightshade. The remains of the lustrous flowers are like paper shreds, but the egg-shaped berries shine brilliantly. Poppies are growing there too, but they are probably the long prickly-headed poppy, Britain's smallest, that grows thickly on this chalky soil. Three partridges scamper along the dusty path beside the meadow, then dodge into the screen of stalks.

1.14. Birds must find the greenfinch a fearful bore as a neighbour. Ever since I stationed myself at this window one has been singing. Singing! Without the faintest hint of experiment, ambition, aspiration, imagination, it has been dully, sluggishly chanting its 'dweee, dweee' note. The sound has all the ennui of late summer in it, much more so than the call of the turtle dove which is always accused of making the August air even more druggedly sleepy. The turtle dove's placid gurgle has none of this bored, lounging indifference in it; it is the articulated passion of a shy and sensitive soul, vibrant with restrained virility.

1.15. Talking of turtle doves, there is one. With all the soft glory of its plumage splendidly revealed to me for a second or two, it flew low and casually across from the shrubberies towards the juniper hedge.

1.29. A mystery has just been enacted. From the extreme left of the Park Field came a round, dumpy form plodding steadily in a straight line across my arc of vision. It was a moorhen. With a curiously humble tenacity it stalked on, like a man advancing under fire, and under orders, across the breadth of the field. Primly, perhaps a little nervously, it ignored the rooks and jackdaws to its left. I watched it for two or three minutes. It must have stepped through the buttercups for five hundred yards while I had it in sight. On the surface there might appear to be little out of the ordinary in that. But here are the facts. Apart from our children's paddle-pool and, in the field corner, a tiny disused, trodden-in cattle pond, no larger than a cartwheel and containing two inches of mud soup, there is no water around here; certainly nothing suitable for moorhens. Nor, until now, have I ever seen a moorhen in the neighbourhood. Where had it come from? And, even more puzzling, where was it *walking* to? For its grimly-pursued track could lead to nothing but a breadth of hilly field, eventually a thin hedge and then more hilly field.

1.43. Within sight from this window is a corner of the children's paddle pool. For the past 20 minutes I have been concentrating on it with my glasses. There has been an incessant coming and going of drinkers and bathers. I have seen six blue tits, three great tits, one marsh tit and one coal tit, many chaffinches, cocks, hens and young, cock and hen greenfinches, two cocks and three hen yellowhammers, two robins, a spotted flycatcher and a willow warbler. At times there was a little ring around the edge, like trippers at Southend determined, with the fierce determination of the practitioners of an unpleasant but sacred rite, to wet their toes with salt sea water. The first cock yellowhammer stolidly *sat* in the water, soaking, like someone enjoying a Saturday night bath. The robins sipped fastidiously without moistening a feather. The blue tits threw themselves in with bustling, boyish pleasure.

1.44. Three young goldfinches have fluttered past the terrace, looking, with their rumpled young feathers and tatty bits of gold braid, something like a party of young Naval lieutenants, scruffy and unshaven after a night out. Immediately after there came over a family of mistle-thrushes, the young ones, in their brilliant mottling and splotching, bright as winged leopards. They leaped like leopards into a rowan tree and began tearing up the berries at a furious pace. Scared by something, they shot away making a noise like the folded cigarette cards that as a boy I used to jam in my bicycle's forks so that they rattled against the spokes.

1.47. Most of the rooks have gone, and the jackdaws too, but the woodpigeons are still there and so are the flycatchers, flipping out occasionally in their fly-murdering dashes. The pied wagtail is back again on the gravel path, and there goes a blue tit, like a little shuttlecock, over to the pool to drink . . .

I returned to my typewriter chastened, purged of the silly feeling that beyond the window was nothing but uneventfulness, and refreshed as if by a draught of water.

Chapter Sixteen

By the time November came the Parfitts were the only people living in the house. The Hobsons had moved away, the Camerons had taken over the empty gardener's cottage, and we had gone into the lodge. The reason for the transfer of the Camerons and ourselves was that under some obscure legal clause the rating authorities dealt more kindly with a house occupied only by caretakers (as the Parfitts now were in name). Bee and I, with the help of other Berewordeans, spent a frightful, exhausting two days moving our belongings from the top floor of the house five hundred yards away to the lodge. After we had begun I hit upon a useful time-and-energy-saving device. Fixed at the window of the Hobson's bathroom was a fire-escape canvas chute. I dragged this out from its dust and darkness, and sent it uncurling out into space. I got my car from the stable, put down the hood, and, driving it onto the lawn, dropped the end of the chute into the back. After that Bee and I tramped to and fro from our room along the passage to the Hobsons' bathroom, tossing articles into the maw of the chute to rocket down into the car. Each time I had a full load we drove down to the lodge, carried the things into there, and then drove back for more.

Once in the lodge life took a happier turn. Hideously baroque and Victorian from the outside, with an omelette of gables and brick turrets, inside it was a comfortable and cosy building. The sitting-room was low ceilinged and had an open fireplace which that winter consumed most of the remaining logs in the rotunda.

Once again we were living as a private family and there were many things I liked about it. It was not all pleasure for Bee. Instead of a three-oven Aga, she had a filthy, ramshackle and maddeningly inefficient range to cook on, and the kitchen was dark and dingy, the only poor room in the house. But during the next few months we got things organized to a smooth routine and, but for the permanently present nightmare of having nowhere to live after this had come to an end, we could have been completely content.

With the memory of the previous year's bacchanalian celebrations still vivid in our minds, Christmas was inevitably palely subdued in comparison. Even so, a number of friends and ex-Berewordeans gathered there, and the hall in the house was brought back into use. There was again a great deal of fun, although, for me, at any rate, it was heavily tinged with nostalgia, and, as one always does on those occasions, I could not prevent my mind constantly switching to that other Christmas and dismally wondering at the unpredictable, unbelievable, changes that had come about in that one year. The inevitable question kept posing itself: Who would have believed it then?

In a curious way life seemed to have taken on a timeless, drifting unreality. Every now and then a prospective purchaser arrived, and – although one wanted the sale to be made quickly – a twinge of fright broke through; but for most of the time it seemed as if we, the Parfitts, Hilary Gardener, the Camerons and Gerald, now the total population of the thirty acres, would continue for ever living this oddly intimate yet dispersed life. The arrival of a prospective was like an invasion of a remote, forgotten land by a foreign explorer. At various times Bereworde appeared, temporarily, to have an odd future before it. It was considered for use as a County Council old people's home, as a training college for Catholic priests, as a headquarters for a little-known cult called the Mazdaznans, as an office block, as a breeding kennels for Alsatians, and as a possible country home for a Swedish film star. The interested came, lost interest when they saw its size, and went. The tedious job of tramping around house and grounds, and reciting Bereworde's wonders and virtues, was under-taken by most of us at one time or another, but usually it fell to Anna.

One Saturday morning I accompanied Anna around with a morose and melancholy little man from a London firm of estate agents, who were placing it on their books. He scraped a jaundiced eye across flaked paint, shaggy grass-edges, dusty outbuildings, and remarked tonelessly: 'Must've been a nice place when it was kept up.' Anna, who, with Bee and Flora, had spent until midnight the previous day putting in order all that three women could put in order in preparation for his visit, maintained a splendid politeness. He was provided with lunch before he left, and then he set off to walk the mile and a half down Pedler's Hill to the bus-stop. A short time later Gerald set off in the Lea Francis to drive into the market town, and caught him up a little way down the lane. He pulled up and offered him a lift. As he screeched into third gear, Gerald said casually, 'What do you think of Bereworde?' Obviously not having noticed Gerald during his tour, the little man said, 'The house is all right, but I've never seen such a queer bunch of people in all my life.'

Once Christmas had gone by it seemed as if we, the tattered little remnant of the community, had rallied for the last time. Perhaps it was that, subconsciously, we had determinedly girded our spirits so that Christmas should be given its due, so that at least it should not be soured for the children. But when the new year took its first gaunt January steps, and there seemed to stretch ahead an eternity of ice-gripped, sulphur-skied days, when day opened reluctantly and night clamped down in mid-afternoon, then our spirits slumped. There seemed nothing, now, to distract Bee and me from the ominous emptiness of our personal future: where to live? where to live? was the unspoken – and often spoken – question that obtruded into everything we did and conversed about. And then, early in the month, at the time that Bee was in University College Hospital having our third baby, while in a nearby ward that anguished and penetrating voice of our times George Orwell lay dying, the news that was at once relieving and dreadful came. Bereworde was sold. A rich industrialist had bought it for a sum which did much to clear away the Parfitts' anxieties.

I should not have told Bee while she was in hospital, but that snow-hurling night when I drove from Fleet Street to see her, I was too despondent to be capable of acting. When she returned to the lodge with the new baby our desperate weekend car-searches restarted. There was an intervening period which probably saved us from going insane from introspection and self-torture: the general election. In the midst of the confusion of the break-up Ian was fighting his campaign, and he needed all the help available. Evening after evening we spent driving and walking around in the wet and cold, knocking on doors and propagating Labour's cause in terms that suggested an inner glowing conviction I personally did not feel. On polling day there was a heartening turn-up of ex-Berewordeans with cars and fountain pens, the Larkins (who had left before we arrived) driving from their farmhouse in Hampshire.

Bee spent the day running a sub-committee room in a cottage front room in a Bedfordshire village, with the five-week-old baby by her side in a carry-cot. I had left London early and spent the afternoon and evening running a car ferry service of remotely-situated voters to the polling booths. At last it was all over. From a dozen different points everyone, fatigued and with rolling empty stomachs, returned to Bereworde. In the big handsome room where we had had so many parties and so many friendly, sprawling, coffee-drinking evenings, Ian was sitting, grey with tension and exhaustion, in the company of Anna and about twenty other people, friends and Labour Party workers. There was not much talk at first while people bit uninterestedly at sandwiches and drank rum, but when the radio results started to come over a shiver of optimism, then jubilation, ran through the gathering as – at first – it seemed that, once again, Labour was going to have a resounding victory.

At about eleven-thirty Bee and I left and went to the lodge. We sat with a corner lamp casting a dim circle of light and the fire flickering around the last log, and we listened to the staccato recital of results. Gradually the cheerfulness increased, for it seemed clear that Britain was not faced with five years of Conservative rule. Ian's figures would not be known until midday tomorrow and I was too tired, too hollow, to stay up any longer.

The next day, of course, the flow of Labour success slowed and Tory wins came through faster and faster, but when Julian telephoned me at the office to say that Ian had got in, my spirits jerked up again.

Yet the election was only a temporary diversion. Once the excitement had died, the same grim, grey pattern imposed itself again upon our lives. The legal convolutions of the sale were slowly but inexorably moving towards the close. We had been told that in six weeks' time we must quit. The Parfitts had fixed their date of departure – to Anna's mother's house, where they were to live until they themselves bought a house. The Camerons went. Gerald arranged to transfer his now one-man business to the market town. The only thing that remained unsettled, and which was apparently incapable of settlement, was our problem.

Then, in the black depths of our depression, exploded an event as fantastic and joyously exhilarating as a Chinese firework. In the post one morning was a letter signed by Helen Rhys, inviting me to a party at which the award of the John Llewellyn Rhys Memorial Prize would be made. I knew, but had almost forgotten, that months ago my agent had entered my first book, *Adventure Lit Their Star*, published the previous year, for the award, and now the letter stated that I was one of the four finalists. The award had been founded by Mrs Rhys in memory of her husband, author of that book of rare vision and beauty, *England Is My Village*, who had died in an RAF aircraft crash during the war. Her intention was to give encouragement and help to young writers, and each year the prize was presented to a writer under thirty whose book was most memorable in promise or in achievement. In my present mood of dejection, the news that *Adventure Lit Their Star* had even reached the final four out of twenty-six submitted was wonderfully stimulating. I did not expect more than that, especially when I learned that another of the four was one of the most brilliant of our younger novelists, whose reputation was already established at a lofty level. I returned with Bee from London a week later in a state of emotional intoxication, for there, before a gathering of writers, publishers and journalists, the award had been made to me.

That was the junction for a turn into a broader and better highway. Only a few days after the award party Bee and I set off on yet another of our cross-country patrols. We drove north-west from Berewode across into Hertfordshire, to visit what had been described in an advertisement as 'a quaint seventeenth-century cottage'. We had visited too many 'quaint seventeenth-century cottages' for me to feel the slightest optimism about what we were about to see. Invariably they seemed to be next to twentieth-century gasometers in slum backstreets of country towns, or so tumbledown as to be remarkable only for the tenacity of some obscure seam of wattle that had kept them relatively upright for so long. Indeed, as we drew to a stop outside this particular antiquity I saw no reason to regret my cynical pessimism. My first impression was of a listing and splintered fence, an ugly porch apparently made from packing cases, walls cloaked voluminously in a matted leprous-coloured creeper except where here and there were gaping holes in the brickwork; and the whole thing far too close to the road. Had I been alone, I think I would have turned the car round and driven back without bothering to get out, but persuaded by Bee's 'we might as well now that we're here' attitude, I swung the car into a trackway and we walked into the jungle that had once been a garden.

It took a surprisingly long time for the truth to percolate through. I became aware that I was thinking 'if that porch was pulled down, those two little oblong windows would be revealed' and 'it's rather nice having a wood the full length of the garden'. We got in through a window, and then Bee and I were racing through the house talking excitedly, swivelling about in the charmingly-proportioned hall with its red tile floor, and exclaiming happily at the lightness and airness of the unexpectedly tall, domed upstairs rooms. Suddenly it was obvious that, with the debris and the clutter and the throttling herbage cleared away by the imagination, this was precisely what we had been looking for, in heavy disguise. And the price? Well, it was formidable but not insuperable, and by post-war standards, low. A few minutes later we were hurrying over to the car and driving at a shuddering top-speed towards the estate agent's office, gripped now by a terror that someone would have beaten us to it – for how could a house with the possibilities of this have stood there so glaringly inviting for more than a day or two?

In point of fact we learned later that the cottage had been standing like that, empty, for three years. During that time the owners had held fast to a price considerably higher than the one we paid for it, but, by happy chance, we had appeared on the scene at the moment that the local authority had suddenly presented the threat of requisition, and the owners had decided to compromise. We had appeared at the moment that the price plunged.

The next few weeks were feverish with negotiations. There were short periods when it seemed that our hopes would break down, but at last the guarantors and the bank, the surveyor and the insurance company, found a common plane of mediation, the completing signatures were scribbled – and we were safe. Given another – and, it was sternly stated, final – extension of tenancy of one month in the lodge, we had time to prepare for the move. The Parfitts, Hilary Gardener, and Gerald packed up and went, but now there was no sense of being abandoned. We waved them goodbye and returned to the lodge to complete our plans: the last Berewordeans.

Chapter Seventeen

Suddenly, with a tranquillity of mind that seemed new and novel, I glanced up from the paperwork and noticed that it was spring again. I walked out of the lodge and strolled across the front lawn towards the rookery grove. How lovely Bereworde looked. It was at that brief moment when the eye encompasses the last of the crocuses and snowdrops and the first daffodils and primroses, and the stars of celandines were beginning to glimmer in the coarse tussocky grass. The wind shook the whippy top branches of the beeches and I could see the tails and beaks of brooding rooks on their nests, riding them like coracles in a choppy sea. Had the rooks noted the diminishing activity of humans around the big house? I wondered – but no, from that height, where the winds were always edged and where the rain struck with unbroken force, where there was all the sky for a view, such a thing as that would be of utter insignificance. The house stretched to my left, its windows blank and curtainless, immersed in an unstirred silence. For the first time I felt physically the queer isolated sensation of being alone there, of knowing the place as no other Berewordean had known it. Now that there was only one more month I would spend every free moment out of the lodge, soaking myself in the atmosphere, I resolved, for it was improbable that I would ever again find myself in the curiously exalted position of having the freedom of such a place – so much space alive with so many untrammelled recollections.

Yet the weeks went ahead in jumps and there were always urgent letters to be written, essential preparations to be made. And the weekend before the removal van was coming, I found myself aware that the time was almost up, that I must be quick. With a pile of dreary documents to be dealt with piled under the glass paperweight – agreements with gas and electricity boards, builders' estimates – I pushed away the typewriter and got up. They must wait. This was the last chance.

I went outside into the richness of a May day bubbling with birdsong, coloured like a carnival. Remorse filled me as I thought of the walks I had never taken, the explorations, planned but never carried out, into the almost unknown country beyond the boundaries. Even the grounds – how often had I *looked* at them? Hadn't they, mostly, been something to pass through on my way to a logging task or a gardening job? Well, there should be a hasty attempt to compensate. First, providing myself with the excuse of making a last check that no belongings had been left in cupboards of our old top floor room, I made for the house.

The side door was open, and I walked up the long passage from the kitchen wing into the hall. In that short time the air had been staled by the musty, dusty aroma of an unoccupied building. The sun slid through the library windows in opaque orange beams, curdling on the empty floors. I stood for a moment before the enormous fireplace of the hall, trying to see it again as it had been on those two Christmasses. Thinly, transparently, I saw them again, the people and the background of firelight and tinsel and ephemeral colour, but it was a strain on the imagination, standing in the sun-drowsy deadness of the lofty room, with the broad staircase twisting up into the hollowness of the upper floors. I mounted the stairs, my footsteps making an uneven clumpity-clump on the bare boards as I limped higher. It seemed odd not to hear the voices of children above. The Parfitts' room had its wooden shutters closed. I went to the centre window and concertinaed the shutters, and as I did there was a fluttering, scraping movement and a bat flipped from beneath the pelmet, then another and another. It was a strange, unreal sensation, standing in the dusky room with the disturbed pipistrelles (for they were the smallest British bat: tiny ruddy-furred mouse-like animals only 3 inches long) swirling about me in fast, silent flight. I stepped into the middle and the bats continued their dizzying criss-crossing patterns, sometimes coming within inches of my head, but, guided by the rebounding of the supersonic vibrations they threw out, they swerved aside at the last second from the obstacle in their path. This seemed to me an almost melodramatic demonstration of the situation: bats had taken possession of Bereworde.

I ignored them and went back to the window. The stepped lawns were whitish in the sun. A green woodpecker was pecking at the gravel of the lower path, nipping up ants, presumably; perhaps woodpeckers had been doing that for years on that path, throughout our time here, in the early mornings before anyone was about; but I had never seen it happening before. A quick movement at the edge of the rhododendron bank down the side of the lawn turned my eyes there and I saw it was a weasel, playing with something trapped between his paws. I had seen the weasel several times around the house during the past month or two, but usually in the vicinity of the Long Wood; once, as I drove down the lane, it scurried across in front of my wheels with a dead baby rabbit held high in its jaws. Yet, again, I had not previously seen it so close to the house. It darted in and out of the rhododendrons several times, a flicker of auburn fur, and then the bush shook and it did not reappear. Everything that my eyes alighted upon seemed to be underlining the desertion of Bereworde, as if wild life, held back to humans for so long, was now lapping forward in an acquisitive tide to take control.

Without going up to our old floor, for I knew there was nothing there I wanted to reclaim, I descended the stairs and went outside. The trembling, flittering song of a willow warbler was in the breeze, and I remembered that I had seen a pair carrying grass and moss into the tangle of nettles and briar near the lodge. As I walked the length of the house along the broadness of gravel that led to the front door, a pied wagtail flew mincingly off. Was it nesting in the drain pipe beside the porch as a pair had done last year. The grass was still marked where the wheels of my overloaded car had churned the soil during the fire-chute moving operation in the previous autumn, but they were being smudged by the growth of stems. Everywhere a shagginess, the beginnings of unkemptness, was spreading, because it was a long time since Ian or Chris or I had sweated as we had steered the bucking, whirring autoscythe across the lawns. Again my mind was flooded by a memory – that of the searingly hot day in June when I had worked naked to the waist drawing into miniature hay stacks the swathes of bleached grass left behind by the autoscythe, and lifting my wooden rake with an unfortunate toad spiked on one of the tines.

My feet took a roving, casual path beside the Italian garden. A hawfinch flew from a yew and I recalled my joy when, using my German naval night-binoculars for the first time at Bereworde, I had picked up the hunchbacked fawn body and the massive bill of a hawfinch at the pinnacle of an ash. No-one was working around the gardener's cottage – it seemed wrong not to see the bent form of Alec somewhere among the vegetables – and silence and secrecy seemed gathered thickest about the ruined cottage, with its crumbled licheny walls. So, after all, after all the ambitious plans sounded loud at family meetings, nothing had ever been done to restore the ruined cottage. I had made a limited effort. I had rebuilt the fireplace in the one sound room and painted the woodwork so as to provide myself with a private work-place, but paper wrinkled with dampness in a matter of hours and I abandoned it. It might have looked different now if the community had accepted the proposal of a writer of moderate fame, who had wanted to patch it up and move in with a companion, but he had suffocated our initial interest in the plan by his incessant and admiring descriptions of his art, particularly of his next book.

I circled back and as I cut behind the derelict tennis court, a grey squirrel ran out of the tree-belt and gained the cover of the shrubberies around the pond by using the boundary fence as a bridge. It went undulating along the top-bar with its tail making a waving motion as it ran, a thing I did not remember having observed before. I followed the squirrel and bisected the Long Wood by taking the hunter's path across its tip. I had another glimpse of the squirrel as it bounded up the trunk of a mature and brawny oak growing over the fence. It was in that oak that I had shot a squirrel on a winter day and I had carried it back to the house to cook it for supper, for I had read that they were good to eat roasted. The skinning of it exhausted me. The thick close-grown pelt did not peel off, glove-easy, as in the case of a rabbit. It had to be dragged back from the flesh, degree by degree. I did not enjoy the meal. I suppose if it had been served to me in a restaurant with an imaginative name attached to it, I would have enjoyed it. But the absurd thought that this was *squirrel* kept intruding, and I became annoyed with myself for being prey to stupid prejudice.

I worked my way up through the edge of the Long Wood and ran into yet another symbol of the uncompleted experiment that Bereworde had housed: a beheaded fir trunk that slanted through the undergrowth, resting on the battered-down fence. Nearly a year and a half ago, on a wild January day, a cyclist had ridden up the drive and interrupted breakfast to report that during the night the gale had thrown a fir across the lane. We left breakfast and trooped out with axes and cross-saw and worked all morning to clear the road. It seemed a generous act of God, because once it had been cut back to the fence and the debris raked aside, there remained a big slab of wood as a valuable addition to the winter stocks. Yet, for one reason or another, all those potential logs had never been claimed. The job had been postponed and ultimately forgotten; now, here was the fir, half-hidden by spring growth, perhaps even the hideout of the resident weasel.

Jackdaws were yapping around the water tower, to which water of gum-aching coldness was pumped from the spring that forced through the chalk marl layer 470 feet below ground. The thump-slosh-thump of the pump was silent. It had been switched off a fortnight ago, and the lodge was being fed by the tank reservoir. As I came towards the iron gates, hung with a decorating firm's board (for on the next day the painters were arriving to give the house a gloss for the new owner) I wondered whether to continue up the lane and beyond the cross roads to the old overgrown gravel pit. It had just that moment occurred to me that nightingales would be back there singing, and during all my time at Bereworde I had been to the pit only three times to listen to them. But no, this last indulgence must be limited to the sentimental journey around the estate. In the lodge was Bee with the children, the luggage, the moving chaos.

I turned on to the drive and again went towards the house in completion of the circle. I walked on to the lower lawn, on to which I had looked an hour before from the Parfitts' room, and stopped. From here I had a full broadside view of Bereworde: the linear brightness of the sun-glazed windows; the warmth of the sun-flushed brick mass against a cornflower sky; the golden weathercock twirling on its mast as it had on the first day we had come to see, so long since; the rise and fall of the rooks' voices beyond. Already, as I stood there in the hot grass, I was excluded, I was one of unnumbered people who had lived in a house of some shape or size on this Eastern Chiltern site called Bereworde, and who had gone. The sadness that I felt was not a falsification of the past for I still had in clear perspective the faults and the disappointments that those two years had held, yet I was aware that many of those defects had roots in my own personality and were part of my own mixed contribution to the community; and, although I could not pretend that they had not existed, their redolence was weaker than that of the friendships, the fun and, yes, the adventure that we had found together here.

While I stood with my thoughts I saw a bird swoop up above the terrace wall, twist on flickering brown wings, and resettle on the children's swing which hung motionless from the limb of a beech. I felt a pulse of pleasure for I recognized the bird. It was a spotted flycatcher, back after a winter away in Africa. Perhaps it had only that day returned for I had not seen it as I passed that way earlier. I stood watching the flycatcher as it made its frequent deadly attacks upon winged insects, returning each time to perch on the swing or the shaky parallel bars along which Andrew had gingerly climbed. The sight of the small, slim bird, with its low, squeaky song, swept away the gathering sadness. The future of Bereworde was something that I had barred from my mind. I would rather by far that it was to be used by the Mazdaznans for their esoteric pastimes, or as a romping ground for Alsatian puppies, certainly as somewhere for old people tranquilly to end their lives, than for its destined purpose. Yet now I saw that really that was irrelevant. Whoever happened to be living out his own idea of life within the walls, whatever particular thing – a carefully reconstructed squirearchy or a rehearsal for world revolution – Bereworde appeared to represent to other humans, the house and its woods and meadows would still be there, the enduring values. The flycatchers would be returning each summer to dart from shadow into sunlight at the passing butterflies.